THE BENJAMIN FRANKLIN LECTURES

OF THE

UNIVERSITY OF PENNSYLVANIA

INAUGURAL SERIES

1948

Lecture Committee

Clark M. Byse
Edgar B. Cale
W. Rex Crawford
Eleanor M. Moore
S. H. Patterson
Theodore L. Reller
David M. Robb
George O. Seiver
Robert E. Spiller
Oma Stanley
Irven Travis
Arthur P. Whitaker
John M. Fogg, Jr., *Chairman*

Editorial Committee

John Stokes Adams, Jr.
Sculley Bradley
W. Rex Crawford
Roy F. Nichols
Robert E. Spiller, *Chairman*

Changing Patterns

In American Civilization

Changing Patterns
in American Civilization

by

Dixon Wecter, F. O. Matthiessen, Detlev W. Bronk,
Brand Blanshard and George F. Thomas
Preface by Robert E. Spiller

Philadelphia
UNIVERSITY OF PENNSYLVANIA PRESS
1949

Preface

THE civilization of the United States has become, during the past few decades, a determining factor in world order—or disorder. Up to the middle of the eighteenth century it could be described as a revolutionary by-product of the civilization of Western Europe and its position of cultural dependence acknowledged; from then until the middle of the nineteenth century it was developing rapidly into self-sufficient independence; in the past one hundred years it has tended more and more to take the initiative in shaping the course of world events.

By this growth it has produced one of the two most powerful of modern nations, and it has developed the only ideology that so far has withstood the theory of the totalitarian state. The peoples who have thus worked out in their experience a successful human order based on the concept of the free individual naturally feel a crusading spirit when they see the old orders of Europe and Asia disintegrating; but when they name their shaping ideology "Democracy" and attempt to explain both it and themselves, they seem to lapse into confusion and contradiction. The American people do not yet understand their own civilization as an accomplished fact.

The causes of this dilemma are complex, but at its heart is the simple truth that the American way is no longer the revolutionary way. It is a tried and established order in which man has discovered for himself a balance be-

tween his needs as an individual and his responsibilities
as a member of society and state. That this result is not
fortuitous can be demonstrated by citing the examples
of countries like Norway, Sweden, Switzerland, New
Zealand, and Australia where the same principles have
been applied to different conditions. Yet the civilization
of the United States is more complex than any of these
and its power greater. We are as distinctive for our con-
tradictions and our inconsistencies as we are for our apparent singleness of purpose.

The inhabitants of this continent are a heterogeneous
mixture of disaffected Europeans, Africans, and Asiatics
who, in a little more than three centuries, have subdued
and put to their uses the resources of a vast and rich land.
Without achieving a racial homogeneity, they have become a recognizable type in a unified nation; without
substantially altering their fundamental assumption of
infinite resources, they have shifted their society from an
agrarian to an industrial economic base; without relin-
quishing their philosophy of political and personal an-
archy on an ideal plane, they have ceased to believe in
revolution.

To defend an established order requires a rationale
different from that which creates revolution, and the
American people have not yet developed a consistent
rationale of order. Self-understanding is the first need,
and self-criticism is the way to understanding. Yet Feni-
more Cooper and Sinclair Lewis were alike condemned
as unpatriotic when they ventured, a century apart, to

question the solid worth of American life. In the eighteen-forties and fifties, the spirit of criticism showed signs of healthy development, and the United States produced a small but mature body of philosophy and literature; but the revolution was not by then complete. Only in the past two or three decades has the critical spirit given promise of defining American civilization as one of the great civilizations of all time in fact as well as in ideal, in achievement as well as in aspiration.

The shift from the ideal to the actual is always painful. It causes doubts and may lead to despair. Mark Twain spoke for the modern disillusioned American when he finally condemned the human race because of an apparent collapse of the moral order. At close range it would some-times seem that we as a people are, like Mark Twain, completely disillusioned. Our literature is somber and violent; our political life is torn by factionalism; our philosophy is pragmatic and materialistic; our religion is diffuse and loosely humanitarian; our total thinking is inclined to be cynical and often sardonic. These phe-nomena, say the thoughtful, are symptoms of decay; but in saying this they express their realistic awareness of facts and their profound concern for values. They are asking us—and we as a nation are beginning to ask our-selves with them—the eternal and always unanswerable questions. History tells us that only at such moments of self-evaluation does man achieve true greatness. The major civilizations of the past have produced tragedies in the hour of their maturity; statesmanship is created by crisis; philosophical comprehension springs from moral revolution. That we, in 1948, are self-critical is our strength.

Such is the spirit which motivated this volume. It is an attempt, in the broadest of terms, to understand and evaluate the civilization of the United States in the twentieth century. It is not a study of our economic resources, our military power, or our foreign policy. It is neither a proclamation of our greatness nor a blast at our materialism and our spiritual weakness. From five points of view—social institutions, literature, science, philosophy, and religion—it asks a single question: Who are we? It seeks to discover the configurations of thought and feeling within which we, both as individuals and as a nation, answer that question daily by our actions. It attempts to make articulate some of the meanings of contemporary American life.

The lectures which are here collected were delivered at the University of Pennsylvania during the spring of 1948 as the inaugural series of Benjamin Franklin Lectures, to be given annually in honor of the founder. The topic was proposed to the University Lecture Committee by the American Civilization Graduate Club of the University, and each lecture was followed by a round-table discussion by the lecturer with the student and faculty members of that club. Publication was an object from the start, and each lecturer was provided with the same set of leading questions to be adapted to his own field of inquiry so that the series as a whole would have a unity of aim and a diversity of means. The book is a single work.

The idea of gathering together a group of informed and inquiring minds to consider a common problem would not seem strange to the man whose name the series bears and who proposed for the American Philosophical Society that membership should represent the various departments of human inquiry. Benjamin Franklin believed always that many minds are better than one, and that truth can be sought best by the comparison of diverse experiences. To honor his memory a lecture series should be planned in the spirit of inquiry rather than of authority; it should consider values as well as facts, and should sacrifice neither one to the other; it should stimulate its hearers to question anew rather than merely to consider the results of past thinking. Both the Lecture and Editorial committees have had these ideals continuously in mind.

Robert E. Spiller

Contents

Chapter   *Page*

    Preface vii
       Robert E. Spiller

  I. The Contemporary Scene 1
       Dixon Wecter

 II. The Pattern of Literature 33
       F. O. Matthiessen

III. Science and Humanity 58
       Detlev W. Bronk

 IV. The Heritage of Idealism 82
       Brand Blanshard

  V. New Forms for Old Faith 125
       George F. Thomas

CHAPTER I

The Contemporary Scene

Dixon Wecter

A YEAR or two ago Bertrand Russell voiced his irritation at being asked, whenever he set foot on our soil, the tourist's perennial question, "And how do you like America?" He professed to find something a little indecent in the query, on the order of "How do you like my wife?" adding that its counterpart was rarely asked of the American in England. The traditional reason for that question seemed wholly to escape Lord Russell. For it is less like asking, "How do you like my wife?"—a wife, whether for good or ill, being a *fait accompli*—and more like an architect's inquiry, "How do you like the house I am building?" Something is taking shape from blueprint to reality. That at least is the American heritage. And when we feel that progress has reached fulfillment, aspiration its dead end, we shall have lost our special character as a people. Also by tradition we have raised the question in a friendly spirit inviting honest criticism, but touched with pride. Britain today, under Attlee and Cripps, is also carrying out blueprints, but the result, whatever its expedients in making the best of a bad plight, is so meager and

1

austere as to suggest makeshift and prefabrication—in which the architect himself feels little or no jubilation. As for another nation of experimental trend, Soviet Russia, the question might be asked, but only one answer permitted.

As for ourselves, we have sometimes asked with a kind of automatic politeness—knowing that, whether we inquire or not, nothing will give the visitor more pleasure than to tell us. This goes on generation after generation. The shrewdness and gusto of Harriet Martineau, the ripe wisdom of Lord Bryce, today find their heirs in Graham Hutton's *Midwest at Noon,* D. W. Brogan's *The American Character,* and the best pages of Harold Laski's *The American Democracy,* while the toploftiness of Mrs. Trollope and Matthew Arnold discover their counterpart in Geoffrey Gorer's recent anthropological study *The American People* and Evelyn Waugh's reports ranging from *The Loved One* to articles in the Luce publications. At times one cannot forbear suspicion that the champagne of these later wits is pressed from sour grapes. The mantle of De Tocqueville has fallen, a little oversize, upon Gallic observers like André Siegfried and André Maurois, whose point of view tends to be more catholic and less rigid than that of the British visitor. A rarer bird is the Soviet critic; a significant difference may be remarked between the only book in this field brought forth by the 1930's, Ilya Ilf and Eugene Petrov, *Little Golden America,* subtitled *Two Famous Soviet Humorists Survey These United States,* and the grim articles for *Izvestia* some months ago by

Ilya Ehrenburg, when, as seemed apparent, there was no time for comedy. In all, we have been surveyed from abroad, measured physically and spiritually, thumped and stethoscoped, by politicians and statesmen, historians, scientists, poets, novelists, even psychoanalysts—the last-named finding that as a group we suffer from regressive infantilism, as proved by our dread of loneliness, our protean symptoms of "momism," and even our addiction to milk as the most popular American beverage.

World-wide curiosity about Americans and their civilization is of course an old one, dating back to the experimental nature of our republic and its basic paradox, so baffling to the Old World, of democracy and free enterprise. What Herbert Croly called the promise of American life has at least undertaken to furnish both security and liberty, and this never ceases to rouse the curiosity, if not the skepticism, of the European mind. Today this interest is vastly heightened by the commanding position of the United States in the future of the whole world—plus the widespread notion that America, with her vagaries of policy, domestic and foreign, her assumption at once of the biggest rearmament and overseas assistance budget and of tax reduction, is the most unpredictable of peoples. Hence this absorbing fascination, this desperate striving by outsiders, to read the riddle set by the Sphinx of the West. To early travelers in the days of her green agrarian youth, America looked and probably was relatively simple —the democracy of Andrew Jackson upon which De Tocqueville reported, or even Chester A. Arthur's American commonwealth analyzed by Bryce. Today, whatever the United States may have or lack, its complexity is visible to all—its racial heritages, pressure blocs, economic tensions, vast cities, and interwoven industrial fabric, along with a technology such as no other people has ever built into its civilization.

The fundamental difference between yesterday and today, in American society, is its interdependence. Our economic mechanism runs fairly smooth, at least so long as lubricated with the oil of prosperity, but its equilibrium is extraordinarily sensitive—in perilous balance between wages and prices, machines and full employment, labor and capital, producer and buyer. Great centrifugal pulls are kept under control only because they match each other. Sudden preponderant strength or weakness within the field of forces can work havoc with the whole. Not our Constitution alone, but our economic machine, operates by checks and balances. It recalls the old Irish custom of tying two goats together before they are let out to graze, under assurance that they will never wander far because they can never agree upon one direction.

The specialization which so fearfully illustrates our interdependence is attendant upon the rise of the city, for urban life inevitably is more integrated, diversified, synchronized, and helpless in the face of crisis than is rural life. A hundred years ago, as we know, this was a nation of farmers. In 1870, even after the great industrial speed-up started by the Civil War, wage and salary workers made up only about half the population of toilers; today they compose more than four out of five. This shift has had many incidental effects, of which the most important is the widespread incomprehension of our urban majority about the problems of a rural minority—notably lack of concern about the five and a half billion tons of soil eroded every year from the face of the nation—or apathy toward other threats in the making, such as recent vigorous attacks by a highly organized stockmen's bloc upon the public lands of the western states. These things, which farmers and ranchmen quickly take in, receive far less public notice than they should because of their apparent remoteness from the world of steel and concrete and asphalt. Yet if we do not preserve our living resources, then the freedom from want, the state of well-being so vital to the growth of democracy, is forfeited.

The specialization which has drastically modified the old self-sufficiency of American life was painfully proved in the Great Depression of the 1930's, the few brief days of the railroad strike two years ago, or to a minor degree the telephone strike of 1947. If factory wheels cease to turn, or communication falters, or the flow of oil or natural gas or electric current suddenly stops, millions are immobilized, areas of acute crisis appear, and great individual hardship if not outright suffering results.

The market crash of 1929 and its aftermath pointed up this interdependence, particularly in the unprecedented calls made upon government. Twenty years ago the average citizen was little aware of the federal authority: it was remote from his daily life and needs and, save for the postman on his rounds, highly impersonal. But under the shock which transformed the mood of that life from plenty to panic, group values altered with astonishing speed. For instance, in retrospect one sees how many changes befell in the winter and spring of 1933, just fifteen years ago: the scrapping of national prohibition, the dimming of a certain glamour surrounding Big Business and mercantile success, a redistribution of power which made Capitol Hill and the White House rather than Manhattan and Wall Street the nation's cerebral cortex, along with new ideas about the functions of government. For the American turned to those dim impersonal forces of which heretofore he had been so unaware. Once the federal power as it affected him had seemed chiefly negative— such as protecting him against foreign armies or foreign competitors, curbing the power of domestic trusts or the adulteration of foods and drugs, and guaranteeing his personal freedom from certain interferences.

Since that time the relation of the citizen to his government has changed markedly. Revolutionary positive steps have been taken as a result of growing complexity and specialization, federal annexations of new fields of social concern, marked developments in the direction of the welfare state. To regard the government as a beneficent friend, an employer to serve, a buckler against economic insecurity, and an umpire to invoke constantly—this attitude, prior to the New Deal, was as unfamiliar to millions of citizens as to other groups was the contrary one of seeing in government an enemy whose power to tax and regulate grew steadily more galling. Before the close of the 1930's, the word "government," referring almost always to Washington, held for Americans of all classes meanings and emotional overtones never possessed before. "My man's working for the government," said the WPA employee's wife proudly; "The government wouldn't let us plant, so we had to go on relief," was a typical hard-luck tale in the cotton belt; "I bought tractors on the money the government give me and got shet o' my renters," declared an Oklahoma landlord; "The hell with the government," growled the Liberty Leaguer in his club. Always it was the government, in those days a synonym for the New Deal.

This extension of social concern and government control came about under three guises, the three R's of the Great Depression—relief, recovery, reform. In terms of relief the New Deal succeeded; about the durability of its reforms I shall speak in a moment. In respect to recovery and employment the New Deal failed, whether in the guise of the Blue Eagle and the NRA, or of the manifold public works programs which did an enormous amount of incidental good but missed their announced target, the revival of industry. The theory, you recall, was known as pump-priming. Our patron saint, Benjamin Franklin, explained it to his sister in 1787: "Sensible people will give a bucket or two of water to a dry pump, that they may afterward get from it all they have occasion for." Its application to economics, in terms of the PWA and WPA, appeared to show that one got out of the pump very little more than the water he poured in, although the gains in civic improvement and individual morale were great. A Gallup poll in June 1939, asking the public to name "the greatest accomplishment" and also "the worst thing" done by the New Deal, found that "relief and the WPA" led both counts by a decisive margin—surely the mirror of a divided mind. Through the power of taxation, the New Deal in effect took from the idle rich to support the idle poor, and in the main, through those days of tension, the nation gave its assent.

Some improvement in economic conditions happened to all nations from about 1933, even as a common disaster had overtaken them from about 1929 onward—so that Americans apparently were not the sole dupes of hit-or-miss prosperity, nor can even a Democrat like me prove that Republicans were the sole villains of 1929 or Democrats the exclusive heroes of 1933. Nevertheless it was the fourth R—rearmament—and the ultimate pump-priming of the Second World War which really ended the Great Depression, and at last sent the long-stagnant pool of eight to ten million jobless citizens to join the brimming floods of full employment. Our first venture in economic resuscitation by federal action must therefore be considered of doubtful success—a sobering thought under the forecast of another and progressively more severe depression in the years ahead, a debacle that certainly will have its chain-reaction throughout the world.

Now the New Deal is buried, along with the leader who

alone was able to hold together its mosaic of factional support. Some of the partisanship of those years still lives —in the periodic stirring of politics, where posthumous hatred of Roosevelt bids fair to become an issue of calculated hysteria like "the Bloody Shirt" of post-Civil War decades. It might be suggested to this opposition that for more effective attack they agree upon an orthodoxy of odium; for example, one school of thought stemming from the Pearl Harbor investigation has proved that Roosevelt was criminally unprepared for Pearl Harbor, while in a book just published Professor Charles A. Beard with equal ease demonstrates that our White House Machiavelli knew about it months in advance and in fact planned it that way. It looks as if some choice will have to be made, between these satisfying but mutually contradictory arguments—although some foes of the late President will want to embrace both, by an ambivalence such as that which the *Chicago Tribune* achieves daily, in abhorring Communism yet fighting all measures designed to check its international spread.

As for domestic politics, beyond doubt the ghost of old factions will linger long. But—and to a social historian this is the significant fact—most of the so-called reform measures of the New Deal have now been built into the durable structure of American government, and are no more likely to be scrapped than the Federal Reserve system which the majority of bankers bitterly opposed prior to 1913. Regulation of the stock market and guarantee of bank deposits, policies of helping the farmer control the output and price of his product, the RFC, the TVA, social security legislation—such are a few of the salient points. Endorsement of most of them in the Republican campaign platforms for the last twelve years, along with the contrast between what Mark Hanna and Joe Cannon would have said about them and the utterances today of such diverse Republicans as Dewey and Stassen—these are arresting signs of change. In politics such ideas have become platitudes. Although Paul Porter, who ran the Democratic campaign publicity in 1944, has lately referred mysteriously to "a four-letter word not spoken in polite company" —spelled, as he presently revealed, T-a-f-t—the Senator from Ohio, for all his conservative temper, espouses a federal program of health, housing, and education considerably more drastic than anything Roosevelt dreamed of in 1932. Thus the drift of our times toward planning and social security.

Indeed, under the vast uncertainties of the world today security has become the foremost desire of millions. Personal economic safeguards have multiplied since the Social Security Act, even though the security of peoples against war and devastation appears to dwindle year by year. Concerning the simpler matter, domestic security, the sociologists Robert and Helen Lynd remarked in the mid-thirties, of their typical town in Indiana: "The most striking difference lies in the emphasis Americans placed, according to Lord Bryce [in 1888], on the adventurous and new in contrast to the emphasis Middletown now places on the tried and safe." Public-opinion polls through the thirties always found youth more friendly than their elders to federal planning, wage-and-hour legislation, curbs upon the accumulation of great wealth, and collective security. "Today's young people want to live, not simply to accumulate," wrote one educator a dozen years ago, remarking that the acquisitive instinct, in terms of fabulous fortunes, was less keen as life's grand objective among the rising generation, who had never heard of Timothy Shay Arthur and rarely of Horatio Alger. Of course they are keenly aware of the importance of being solvent—children of the Great Depression could hardly be otherwise—but many regard the pyramiding of great wealth as no longer feasible. Whether for this or more idealistic reasons, a subtle change has occurred since the 1920's, when most undergraduate males (at least in the major eastern universities) dressed like budding stockbrokers. "You can't take it with you" is more than the title of a once-popular play about a happy-go-lucky family that picnic through life. Under the rising tide of wars and rumors of wars in the atomic age it has a more than usual relevance. You may recall one of Bill Mauldin's recent cartoons showing a toothless old millionaire, stooped and purblind, a champagne glass before him and a bevy of chorus girls at his elbow, gloating, "I've made my pile— now I'm gonna enjoy it!"

Beyond doubt the revulsion against this attitude can go too far, whether it lead to hedonism or lack of enterprise. Anthropologists tell us that among the Zuñi Indians it is considered bad form to pursue personal ambition—so that the man of initiative is regarded as a sinister fellow, and punished, while the desire for power, distinction, achievement, fades into a twilight of mediocrity and sloth. Such conformity to the group ideal, by the way, is striking proof of the extent to which human nature is malleable, and its behavior patterns subject to change. On the other hand, in prosperous times like the present, the competitive spur of American life tends to reassert itself—although the present is one postwar era in which material abundance has not bred the complacency from which the nation suffered in the Gilded Age or the Harding administration.

To return to the mind of youth, at least among the rank and file, one observes a more modest expectation of fortune, a desire for a living wage, fair prices and controlled profits, and social security, accompanied by a trend toward earlier marriages less intent upon the old Victorian pledge of supporting the bride in her accustomed style, and more upon the salvaging of whatever happiness is possible from the world's dark uncertainties. One important fact is that nearly half of all American families have some member who is a veteran of the Second World War. The benefits of the GI Bill and services of the Veterans Administration —ranging from higher education and loans for housing to free medical care for nonservice-connected disabilities—all tend toward a measure of socialization, for a segment of the citizenry, such as Britain is now attempting for the whole.

Indeed, throughout Western Europe the war accelerated

the drift toward socialism. On the other hand, while Russia grows internally more conservative, her exportable product ministers to desperation. Whether the wavering nations will accept our positive aid in building themselves back to prosperity, or Russia's negative appeal to their misery, is of course the question of the hour.

Let us not flatter ourselves through misunderstanding the average European's attitude. He is more interested in our material production, food, and machinery, and still more in our military potential against communism, than in the ideas and ideals which interest us as Americanism. Weary, impoverished, a prey to fear and disillusion, he is not much engrossed in the theory of democratic capitalism or what we call "free enterprise," or somewhat better, "private enterprise." If captious, he might even venture to ask on the one hand why the Marshall Plan for economic recovery should not be implemented by private funds, with investors and entrepreneurs taking all the risks in the classic manner—or on the other hand, if we find the project too big for free enterprise at home, why many of our congressmen should boggle at a considerable degree of socialization in the means of its expenditure abroad? Our replies on either horn of this dilemma might also be a little embarrassing, the first to the European and the second to ourselves. First, that our private investors would not consider him a very good risk in terms of ledger profits, whatever the enormous gains in other ways if we win this gamble. Secondly, that too many Americans cannot tell their friends from foes, suspecting even middle-

of-the-roaders like Mr. Attlee (a "sheep in sheep's clothing," in Churchill's phrase) as a radical, and thus
unwittingly helping our sworn enemies, the Communists,
in the perfection of their camouflage.

To speak of the hazards of the Marshall Plan is not to
lose heart. It stands in the great tradition of American
generosity and idealism, an idealism which serves as
counterpoise to our temptation to grow smug because of
our prosperity and power, or immersed in what the ancient Greeks called *hubris*. A public health official lately
termed obesity "the great American dietary problem,"
while radio voices hawking nostrums that bubble and
fizz tell us what to do "for that unpleasant feeling of
fullness"—afflictions which in most sectors of the world
would evoke scant sympathy. The obverse side of the
American character, its liberality, helpfulness, and old-
fashioned frontier neighborliness, cannot and must not be
allowed to lapse, nor on the other hand the idealism of
the Marshall Plan presented without its very real ingredi-
ent of enlightened self-interest or its relation to the en-
forced brotherhood of man which the world is beginning
tardily to concede. A Gallup poll in March 1948 showed
that two-thirds of the American people want a stronger
United Nations. Whether the United Nations will prove
to be Utopia or myopia, the next few months will surely
determine.

To a great extent, the immediate pattern of world
events will be settled within our own domestic framework.
Either a revulsion toward isolation or a lapse into some

major economic depression could undo everything. Let us admit that our so-called "American way," with its large freedoms, its prodigality, its fierce individualism, is not the marching step of the world majority—and the only logic which can ever persuade others to imitate us is our continued practical demonstration of its success. The world, we may be sure, is watching us, just as it scrutinized the United States in the throes of a civil war, when Lincoln kept reminding his people that if the Union failed, the dawn of democratic hope would be blotted from other skies around the world. Moreover, is an American democracy bound by limited desires for security and socialization likely to replace the elder democracy which exulted in free enterprise and individualism, extravagance and optimism? This question is yet unanswered.

To return, then, to the domestic picture and the model which it offers for imitation or rejection. What is the configuration today of our social institutions? The place of woman is plainly one of the key facts, determining not only the shape of marriage, the home, and upbringing of children, but also much of the country's economic and political texture. The Department of Labor lately noted that women compose twenty-eight per cent of our postwar labor force, constitute fifty-one per cent of the voting population, own seventy per cent of the wealth, and make eighty per cent of the purchases. It is little wonder that visitors often call our civilization a matriarchy. The day of the embattled suffragette seems as quaintly outmoded as the hobble skirt, along with its pose of truculent defiance. "Women today are much less consciously women citizens, more consciously citizens," writes Kathryn Stone of the League of Women Voters, remarking that the first symposium of that group, held in 1920, addressed itself to such topics as "Women in Industry," "Child Welfare," and "Civil Status of Women," while today a typical program pivots about atomic energy, full employment, and world government. The so-called equal-rights amendment, favored by some groups to remove the last legal barrier to complete equality, is opposed by the League of Women Voters and some of the nation's foremost women, including Eleanor Roosevelt, deeming it to jeopardize the protection of women in industry and certain legal rights such as alimony. Complete parity between the sexes before the law, it is charged, may outrage biology as well as betray woman's own best interests. Not very long ago the centennial of the first women's rights convention at Seneca Falls, New York, was celebrated in the auditorium of the Labor Department in Washington. As reported by the press, the tone was one of gratification, tempered by mild nostalgia in finding so few worlds left to conquer. The Dean of Vassar even exulted that the saloon was no longer man's castle: "Whom does he find with feet on the brass rail beside him? Woman!" Indeed, whispers of reaction could be heard, including one speaker's forecast that community-cooked meals will never take the place of the family kitchen because "too many women find creative satisfaction in cooking." From the Census Bureau's announcement that nearly four million babies were born in 1947, it was also evident that motherhood had not been alarmingly renounced as a career.

The President of Oberlin College recently told of a lone woman sitting on a board of trustees who persistently objected to measures dear to the chairman's heart, until finally he burst forth, "Madam, why, oh, why did God create women so beautiful—and so dumb?" "I can answer that," she said quietly. "He made us beautiful so that you would love *us,* and dumb so that we could love *you.*"

Some of the older concepts of marriage, including the firm anchorage of women in the home; double standards in education, morality, and professional opportunity; the stern dominion of husband and father; high birth rate and low divorce—all have been altering more rapidly in the United States during the past half century than in any other nation. This change is now having repercussions, whether for good or ill, among other cultures as widely different as those of Britain and Japan. The sum is probably a mixture of good and ill, with good predominant.

We need not grieve over the disappearance from the United States—save among immigrants not yet assimilated, and some rural households—of the old family hierarchy, headed by the autocratic father dispensing rewards and punishments, fancying himself Jehovah, but often a tiresome old bore. Surely we need not pine for the vanished abuses bred by the double standard, or, in another sphere, for the unending drudgery now banished from the home—soapmaking, pickling, preserving, canning, bread-baking, herb-brewing, dyeing, clothmaking, and the like. These skills, still known to rural families in the Old World, have largely been taken over by specialists outside the home. Even the tin can is in retreat before the frozen-food package, while bread arrives not only baked but sliced. Neither the electric washing machine nor lately the "washeteria" (where laundering becomes again a communal rite, as on the banks of the Po and Ebro) has seriously checked the march of the professional laundry. Electricity has largely supplanted servants as well. Even during the first quarter of the twentieth century, as Chicago's Professor Ogburn finds, the number of domestics fell fifteen per cent, while the number of restaurants increased four times as fast as the population. Today less than one household in twenty employs any domestic help. The widespread American preference for vacuum cleaners and electric dishwashers as against servants may outrage old aristocratic ideas of a privileged class, but has certainly fostered a broader base for the democracy of leisure. This preference of course can exist only within the frame of a highly technological civilization, and abroad, in both Europe and Asia, labor by the sweat of the brow generally remains still cheaper than machines.

More dubious for imitation is the rapidly growing

divorce rate, an American phenomenon publicized through the world by our movies and the polygamous stars they glorify. (Movies, we might add, which exalt "romance" as the exclusive end of marriage—furthermore, a cinema product built as a world of escape from average American life, but accepted abroad, ironically enough, as a faithful mirror of that life.) In 1900 only one American marriage in twelve ended in shipwreck. Now the casualty rate stands at one in five, well over half a million couples annually; among war marriages a ratio of one in three is reported, while in some metropolitan areas (such as Dallas County, Texas) divorce tends to outrun marriage. As we know, the city exceeds the farm, the West tops the East, and the East the South—not only because lax divorce laws attract the discontented, but because dissolution of the bond is favored by a mobile population, freed from ties of family and neighborly opinion. "Annulment" also grows in favor, among those whose grounds for legal divorce are flimsy. No society in history has shown so widespread a shift in so short a time. In ancient Rome of the civil war era, the first century B. C., marked symptoms of family disintegration, chiefly among the leisure class—divorce, refusal to bear children, infidelity, and other symptoms—led to the Julian legislation and an era of stern enforcement, stressing the civic obligations of marriage, parenthood, and family cohesion—laws not repealed until the fourth century after Christ and soon thereafter supplanted by the Christian code of Basil.

Ending an unhappy marriage is, to most Americans, less regrettable than the ugly causes that lie behind it, such as bickerings and recriminations within the home. Their roots are too complex for discussion here, ranging from economic vanities like keeping up with the Joneses and the sumptuary appeal of advertising ("Your Home Is Not a Home Unless It Is Changing," proclaims a Marshall Field caption in Chicago) to those emotional instabilities aired by psychoanalysis, recent discussions of modern woman as "the lost sex," and the chasm between male theory and practice lately explored by the Kinsey Report, actually titled *Sexual Behavior in the Human Male*. Whether we approve or not, the marriage institution and the code of personal behavior are undergoing pretty extensive changes or elastic accommodations, both at home and abroad. An anthropologist might regard the trend as needed modification of old habits to a new social climate and living patterns—like tribal excursions into polygyny and polyandry, or the medieval dissociation between love and marriage—from which society will sometime return (as has been its wont) to stricter monogamy.

Despite the present higher birth rate, which always heralds mobilization and follows demobilization—today shall we take our choice?—the huge families of old are clearly obsolete. Ideas of limitation have been too deeply ingrained. What the 1900's called "race suicide" and the 1920's "birth control" has now become, by a singular triumph of semantics, "planned parenthood." While neither the housing shortage nor the shadow of atomic war serves to daunt the valor of reproduction, on the other hand in the quantitative mass the smaller family is here to stay. For the individual, it means greater freedom but less richness of family structure and delegated responsibility. Some critics of the small city family insist that in comparison with the old prolific tribe it is a seed-plot of neurosis, selfishness, and undue forcing of the child toward precocity and worldy success. (As somebody has observed, the modern couple with so few children have no margin for error, as did the parents of larger broods.) If this charge is true, the egocentrism of the modern family may work some influence upon the national character. A former social worker inquired not long ago in the *Atlantic Monthly,* "How can there be successful international relations, enlightened world government, or any world peace as long as society is made up of millions of ingrown, completely self-interested families? How can such families produce citizens who can change a world psychology from murderous rivalry to rational co-operation?" Here, as in so many adjoining fields, the problem is to reconcile individualism with the social obligation.

Another key fact in the configuration of our social institutions today is the altered position of labor in our highly industrial society.

A signal gain of the past twenty years has been the retreat of child labor. While an amendment to the Constitution pending since 1924 still languishes short of ratification, the NRA of fifteen years ago and more durably the Fair Labor Standards Act of 1938 have abolished most areas of abuse, except in the rural South. In the field of adult labor, the past two decades have seen a sharp swing of the pendulum toward unprecedented strength for organized labor, then an oscillation back toward center with the Taft-Hartley Act of 1947. As one surveys these years, it is clear that labor's bid for power is not purely an economic question or political, but in large measure a quest for simple prestige—to compensate for the dull impersonal grind of assembly-line methods, the loss of creative satisfactions vanished with the handicrafts of an earlier day, along with the diminished chance for individual advancement from rags to riches. An allied demand is the right to leisure—one of the newer rights articulated under the growth of the democratic idea. In fact, in the climate of the New World the individual's political rights have been quicker to burgeon than his social rights. In respect to hour-and-wage legislation, workmen's compensation, unemployment insurance, and old-age security, the United States, as we know, was long outpaced by the Scandinavian countries, Britain, Australia, and New Zealand. Only when a nation has reached limits of physical expansion, exploited its frontier, mined its virgin land and timber, does it apparently start to take legislative thought for the more modest plums of a steady job, leisure for beer and skittles, provision against the hazards of age and illness.

Labor's loss of individual incentive is one by-product of our industrialization with its nurture of cities. The age of the steam engine had a powerfully centripetal effect, in agglomerating the people into huge cities required by the new tasks of industry, resulting in painful congestion. But that of the internal combustion engine, joined to the electrical era, has luckily had the opposite trend— diffusion—tending to separate the spot where one works from that where he sleeps and plays. For some years the fringes of cities have been growing much faster than their cores. The mounting volume of traffic, pouring into the canyons of Metropolis each morning and debouching upon the hills and dales of Suburbia at dusk, testifies to this change and also poses new problems in speed and regulation. The dilemma of the future seems to lie between the highwayless town, its residential zones barred to major travel, and the townless highway, with under- and over-passes for arterial crossings. As overseas critics have been remarking since the youth of Henry Ford, the American at the wheel is the centaur of the machine age, and the social effect of the automobile upon his life and habits hard to exaggerate. To his car the average American clings with wistful tenacity—in the Depression, when very few new cars were sold but filling-station business doubled in volume, and in the late war, when he often had a nice shiny car but not enough gas to run it—for the automobile has become a precious symbol of mobility, freedom, recreation. The scattering of population begun by the epoch of fast motorcar and superhighway seems to fit with the ominous blueprints of the atomic age, and the new dispersal of industry which is now a major defense headache.

Community planning has its ideological side. You recall L'Enfant's design for the city of Washington, with its radial avenues and circles whose approaches could be commanded by artillery against the rise of the commune. And recently Charles Ascher, official of the National Housing Agency, observed that every city of the future should provide "a great square in which to hold civic demonstrations. . . . In Moscow and every provincial town designed by the Soviets [they] have their Red Squares for parades and public affirmations of loyalty. Then there will be no arguments between the police and groups trying to march up the main business street, turning into charges of suppression of free speech." One skeptic ventures to doubt that Red Squares are in any sense equivalent to Union Squares and Hyde Parks—in fact the gulf between them is one of the most important in the world.

In the face of these changes, how much of the time-honored ideal of American freedom of life have we been able to salvage and preserve? The President's Civil Rights Committee has recently expressed "the conviction that no nation in history has ever offered more hope of the final realization of the ultimate ideal of freedom and equality than has ours." The infinite worth of the individual person, his liberty, dignity, and integrity, is the core of our political inheritance—stemming largely from the conviction that all souls are equally precious in God's sight. Having this large enfranchisement, the individual is free to be different, within the framework of the common welfare, and should by the same token regard other men as not only his peers but comrades. This is a nobler ideal, a surer touchstone of what we like to call Americanism, than the aforementioned economic corollary of free enterprise, "the fifth freedom" of which some conservatives made too much during the war, principally for its nuisance value. The privacy and the responsibility of the individual is more basic, and also less flexible to party distortion, since its essence is social conscience, the will to coöperate, understanding and love. Those who never trespass upon the integrity of others are entitled to free enterprise; otherwise that phrase may become a mask for selfishness and license. As Henry Alonzo Myers of Cornell points out, in his cogent little book *Are Men Equal?* the doctrine of equality, not in mind or body or talent, but equality of all men in ultimate worth, is the only doctrine which is really tenable. The essence of the notion of superiority, like any form of evil, is separateness. And separateness is destructive, its fruits being unawareness, lack of social perception and feeling, stupidity and hatred. This of course is one of the reasons why communication, discussion, and free criticism are required if a nation's people are to realize democracy among themselves, and vital if they are to reach understanding with the people of other nations.

The shape of American life ought to offer the world a model for safeguarding essential rights—which elsewhere in the world are either abrogated by the "monolithic" state or else exist in weak countries only upon sufferance by their dominant neighbors. These rights include freedom of belief and worship, opinion, speech, and assembly; fair trial and protection from arbitrary arrest; property rights; education; the right to a job, food, clothing, and housing; social security; franchise; and equal protection under the law. They were implicit from the beginning of the Republic, but have taken shapes not always clearly foreseen by Jefferson or Madison. Yet the taproot was there from the start—that democratic individualism, the coöperative spirit that knitted together the disparities of thirteen states and a variety of economic and regional interests. A wholly modern application of this idea of democratic coöperation is seen, for instance, in the new regionalism, unrolled these last fifteen years along the Tennessee and Columbia River valleys. Statesmen and politicians, in drawing boundaries on their maps, have always thought of rivers as natural walls of separation, whereas their practical effect is to unify the interests and enterprises on both sides of the stream. As somebody has said, regionalism has no boundaries, only centers. Although such planning looks always to the greatest good of the greatest number, it has been saved from the fanatic do-gooders, the theorists of social engineering, by its spirit of voluntarism and its grass-roots responsibility independent of Washington. As David Lilienthal has said, the TVA offered a real contribution to the philosophy of government at a time when, in order to curb the centralization of industrial and financial power, government itself had taken rapid strides toward centralization and might in turn develop the pathology of power. Perhaps such regionalism prefigures the possibility of wider coöperation in the shadow of atomic developments achieved, ironically, by the huge hydroelectric potential of Oak Ridge and Hanford. If the Tennessee and Columbia, and potentially the St. Lawrence, then why not the Rhine and the Danube? The recent fusion of the Benelux nations and the fifty-year economic and military alliance called Western Union promises a new European regionalism overstepping traditional boundaries that have bred so much weakness and mischief. Whether the American public will soon be ready for a still greater experiment on coöperation, world government—now favored by one in four citizens, according to Roper and Gallup polls, in comparison with one in five a year ago—will be determined largely by future events.

Here at home the application of democratic good will has plenty of room for improvement. What economic barriers were to the social conscience of the mid-thirties— the "third of a nation ill fed, ill clothed, ill housed"—race discrimination and prejudice have become to the latter forties. Best-selling novels, plays, movies, scholarly books like Gunnar Myrdal's and those of lighter weight like Carey McWilliams', radio discussions, fair employment practice legislation and the report of the President's Civil Rights Committee whose acceptance by Mr. Truman split the Solid South on the eve of a presidential election—all are proof at least that the older complacency and its conspiracy of silence have ended. In respect to the Negro— one American in every ten—progress has been irregular. In the armed forces, the edge of discrimination is only a little blunted, and murmurs of mutiny grow louder under the new Selective Service Act. In organized labor, much improvement shows; the distinguished Negro educator Charles S. Johnson calls it "the biggest single forward surge of Negroes in the main stream of American life in the past ten years." In major league baseball and intercollegiate athletics, on the staffs of some large city hospitals, in interracial churches and schools, and the faculties of some twenty-five white colleges—a growing disposition is seen in some areas to treat with individuals rather than with pigmentation. And—as significant a detail as any— the younger generation in most communities is more tolerant than the elder. In an extended discussion of race prejudice in the Gary public schools, for instance, students agreed that it was hopeless to try to educate their parents. Symptoms of the revolt of youth have rarely been more heartening.

On the other hand, signs of increased discrimination also appear. The one and a quarter million Mexicans and their descendants, mostly in Texas and California, who tend to be barred from restaurants, movies, hotels, ele-

mentary schools, and the like, have long offered one of the
most vulnerable spots in our Good Neighbor Policy with
all Latin America. One of my ablest graduate students at
the University of California, a Japanese American who
served in uniform throughout the war, after months of
search has been unable to find any kind of professional
employment and lately moved to Hawaii in hopes of
better luck. The National Community Relations Advisory
Council, studying over a hundred private employment
agencies in ten cities in 1946, found that nine out of ten
included religion on their questionnaire, and still more
strikingly that in eight major cities, among discriminatory
help-wanted ads in the press, an over-all increase of 195
per cent occurred between the years 1945 and 1946. Widespread reports of anti-Semitism indicate that the bacterial
warfare so zealously manufactured by Hitler and scat-
tered to the world leaves its spores behind. It seems clear
that almost every individual, like every section and nation,
carries the dormant virus within him, and only decency's
innate powers of resistance can keep such germs from
multiplying. As a student of Mark Twain I have thought
repeatedly of his dictum, "Jews are members of the human
race. Worse than that I cannot say about them." At
present, as we all know, discrimination against any racial-
origin group in the United States has its echoes in some
motherland overseas, while the Negro is of universal concern to the dark-skinned peoples of the earth. Those who
try to prove our democracy a sham, and our professions

of faith empty, find no better weapon than this. We often hear that we cannot escape history; it is equally impossible to escape world opinion.

"Democracy substitutes self-restraint for external restraint," wrote Justice Brandeis a quarter-century ago. "It demands continuous sacrifice by the individual and more exigent obedience to the moral law than any other form of government." The hold of the moral law upon the American people is still apparent, despite shifts in group morals and the slow wane of institutional religion, traditional keeper of the ethical shrine. Among the churches, sectarian jealousy has definitely lessened—certainly since the times of Increase and Cotton Mather, probably since those brave pioneering efforts toward tolerance, as symbolized by a marble plaque still found over the door of the Church of Christ at Vernon, New York, built in 1821: "Free for any People to Worship God in, when not occupied by the Baptists." Mergers and interchurch coöperation are more common today than ever before. And, while churchmanship seems gradually to dwindle in zeal if not in numbers, religion as an inner experience—fruition of America's long tutelage to the Protestant spirit and, one might add appropriately in this city of Philadelphia, to the numerically small but powerful example of the Quakers—continues probably much less impaired. Whether one appraises the popularity of novels by Lloyd Douglas or books like *Human Destiny* and *Peace of Mind,* or at a more austere level the following of Reinhold Niebuhr, one meets the group hunger for clarification and understanding. The inner realities of religion belong to another lecture in this series. It is sufficient here to point out the constantly growing social interpretation of the Gospel, and the endurance, within and without the shell of dogma, of the light of Christian brotherhood. Whether this spirit can find the necessary social implements, at home and among the nations, to save mankind from selfishness, cruelty, disintegration, and suicide still remains to be seen.

I was struck the other day by a passage in the letters of the late George E. Woodberry, Columbia University's humanist of a generation ago. "I wonder," he wrote to a friend in 1918, "if the world is not approaching a series of 'great wars' of which this is only the first, due to science and human ineptitude for great power suddenly acquired (as in the *nouveaux riches*). . . ." Is not modern man precisely that: a parvenu of physical power?

In the beginning I mentioned the obvious but basic fact that our American civilization is deeply, delicately interdependent. It is equally plain that in these times of quick communication, whether of hope or dismay, good will or hate, the nations of the earth are also interdependent. Like mountain climbers, they are roped to each other in the bonds of treaties and working agreements, loans and debts, the abundance of one which complements the needs of another. Prosperity, security, and peace are likewise interconnected and, in truth, a fabric indivisible. The commonalty of man and the commonweal of nations march together. For, unless an atmosphere of democratic serenity and security prevail, no social change for the better, no program of group achievement, can well be undertaken. Under the tensions of anxiety and repressive fear, such changes as occur are apt to be deterioration— that is, shaped by prejudice, violation of civil rights, mob violence and hysteria—manifestations of the herd huddled together in panic. The future of American social institutions therefore pivots as never before upon the future of the whole world.

CHAPTER II

The Pattern of Literature*

F. O. Matthiessen

To GENERALIZE upon anything as complex as the literary scene with which we are surrounded, we must view it with some detachment. Otherwise we shall see many crowding details, but we shall hardly discern a pattern.

One mode of detachment might be to look first at American literature as it impresses Europe now, because now, in a way that would not have been true a generation ago, American literature is much read in Europe. And if we note which of our books are having a vogue there, we can perceive two phenomena. You may have observed that writers from continental Europe, particularly from France, who have visited this country in the years since the war, have met the inevitable interviewer at the dock with: "Oh yes, you have four great authors in America— Hemingway, Faulkner, Steinbeck, and Caldwell." It seems always to be that list, as though there were no others, and as though these were all equal. But no matter

* When I gave this lecture, my travel journal, *From the Heart of Europe,* had not yet been published by the Oxford University Press, so I adapted some paragraphs from it.

how odd that list may seem to us, if we consider these four authors together I think we can see that, despite all their differences in talent and significance, they do have something in common: a preoccupation with violence. And there is a paradox, a haunting paradox, that America, spared so far the worst violences of fascism and war close at hand, has imagined violence in a way that has compelled Europe's attention during its time of terrible destruction. To be sure, the violence in these four authors is not just imaginary. It rises from what Hemingway and Steinbeck have observed in various parts of our country, and from what Faulkner in particular has projected out of the southern past into the present: the violence that may yet destroy us all. Another reason why these writers have been read so much in France is the naturalistic directness with which Hemingway in particular has handled his material. This has given many European writers a new technical resource, a way of breaking through their own more complex literary traditions to raw experience.

The other phenomenon is more confusing. If you go through the bookstores of Paris, or of almost any other European capital now, you will see everywhere translations of our recent best sellers, no matter how bad. The reasons for the popularity of one of the more respectable among them, *Gone With The Wind,* are, I suppose, much the same in Europe as they are here, especially its easy way of telling a moving story. And in translation, lack of distinction in style is always less evident. Still it is startling to learn that this novel brought big prices on the black market during the Occupation. It was read as a resistance book. That is a very baffling reversal of values when you recall that during the war treated in *Gone With The Wind* —no matter what sentimentalizations in its account —the states that were occupied should have been occupied. It happened to be a war about slavery.

It is even more startling to hear that in Budapest a year ago, in a kind of Hungarian Gallup poll, *Gone With The Wind* was voted the most popular book in all foreign literature, past or present, with *War and Peace* considerably behind. As I talked to various people in Budapest, the reasons seemed to boil down to something like this: In such a book Europeans now find a product of the new America that they are going to have to reckon with, a symbol of the large American expansiveness, whether in print or in technicolor.

With a book like *Forever Amber* it is a different story. When France, with its unparalleled heritage of salacious literature, betrays it for ersatz *Amber,* we have arrived at the uneasy epoch when Europeans, like ourselves, have been forced by the speed of journalistic communication to read so much and so fast that a book is no longer something to be dwelt on with care, but rather a bright blurred symbol calling for a quick response. Seen from across the Atlantic, such best sellers can tell us, even more clearly than when we notice them at home, the increasing conquest of publishing by mass production, with consequent standardization. We have reached the point where the next best seller could be turned out on the assembly line.

It really could be assembled rather than written. There could be in the publisher's office in New York one room for history, where it could be decided whether the modes this year favored seventeenth-century Restoration England or nineteenth-century Frontier America. There could be another room to work out how far the love interest might go, and still another where they dubbed in the dialogue. And naturally there would be a special beauty contest to decide who should appear in the advertisement in *Publishers' Weekly* as the author of the book, so that it would be sure to sell.

These best sellers, the latest infection that we have given to Europe, are put together with both eyes on Hollywood. This is of concern to us as readers of literature because, as James T. Farrell has been pointing out so trenchantly, there has been an immense effect now from Hollywood back upon our fiction. Farrell is one of the most serious moralists dealing with American taste today. He applies very searching standards and finds that in the last fifteen years in particular there has been increasing corruption in our fiction as it has looked toward the quick response to the scenario. One can trace that even with a serious writer like Steinbeck. Much of his narrative since *The Grapes of Wrath,* particularly in *The Moon Is Down,* has fallen virtually into scenario form.

These two very different phenomena can both bring home to us the problem of the audience in a time that has come to speak in terms of mass civilization and minority

culture. They can serve to point up the differences between the official version of our life and its actual quality.
By the official version I mean that given by promotion
literature, by spread-eagle orations, by sales talk, by slick
propaganda, by the obsessive development of advertising
techniques, by the phony standardized version in the news
magazine. Some of these are hardly new devices in America, but they have become increasingly rampant during
the past quarter-century. It is the function of the artist to
cut through the official to the actual, and whenever the
artist feels himself oppressed by the official version of life,
he feels himself alienated from his society. You do not
have to look very far in American literature to perceive to
what an extent alienation from society has been the per-
current theme of our time.

With this criterion of the function of the artist, I want
to attempt a further description of the pattern we find
ourselves enacting. In dealing with literature, one is always making a qualitative rather than a quantitative
investigation; and in estimating the writers of one's own
time, one is peculiarly liable to make mistakes. I am
obviously not attempting an inclusive account of all the
writing being done in America today. I take solace in the
kind of qualitative selection I am giving by remembering
that of the writers around whom we now construct our
image of the greatness of our mid-nineteenth century,
none of them were best sellers within their lives. Not
Hawthorne, or even Poe. Certainly not Thoreau, or Mel-

ville. It was Longfellow who was the popular poet, not Whitman.

The tendency now is to describe our recent literature by decades, which often forces a pattern rather than perceiving one that is actually there. Yet the habit is almost inescapable inasmuch as 1919, 1929, 1939—the postwar year, the year of the stock-market crash, the prewar year— each marks an end and a beginning. It was fashionable in the nineteen-thirties to speak of a complete break with the twenties, to refer to the twenties as a time of evasion and escape, of the thirties as a time of renewed social responsibility.

That generalization now looks much too simple as far as the twenties are concerned. We can now see that decade as one of great variety and fertility. To confine ourselves at first to fiction, the year 1920 was signalized by the appearance of *The Age of Innocence, Main Street,* and *Poor White;* and when you recall those three novels, you are aware at once of immense differences both in content and in methods. Edith Wharton, the follower of Henry James, was evoking the manners and standards of an older New York, whereas Sinclair Lewis and Sherwood Anderson were both confronting the crude facts of the new middlewestern small towns, though with marked disparity in what they found there.

The twenties were a period of fresh beginnings and a period when America became conscious of talents which had long been ripening. Willa Cather and Ellen Glasgow were by no means new writers during that decade, but a good deal of their best work was done then. Ring Lardner began to be fully appreciated for his masterful handling of the American language. Theodore Dreiser, the great opener of doors for other writers, as Anderson called him, reached his widest audience with *An American Tragedy* in 1925—a quarter of a century after the initial suppression of *Sister Carrie*. In 1925 there also appeared *In Our Time* and *The Great Gatsby,* Hemingway's first collection of stories and Scott Fitzgerald's strongest novel.

By 1930 there had begun to be a shift in emphasis. It was the year of John Dos Passos' *42d Parallel*. Dos Passos, of the same age as Hemingway and Fitzgerald, was embarked on a more detailed political, social, and economic study of America. His trilogy, *U.S.A.,* completed with *1919* and *The Big Money,* was the most sustained effort of the period to record recent history. But 1930 was also the year of *As I Lay Dying*. *The Sound and the Fury* had appeared in the previous year. These books inaugurated the series in which, as many critics now begin to realize, William Faulkner was to give his reading of a whole region and to establish himself as one of our few serious historical novelists, as he studied the terrible burden of the past upon the present in the Deep South. Thomas Wolfe, whose period of vast and often formless production also coincided with the thirties, wrote a more personal history. But by his death in 1938 he had also begun to be caught up by the same events that were absorbing most of the other new writers of that decade. *Young Lonigan* in 1932, Farrell's first book, and *In Dubious Battle* in 1936, perhaps Steinbeck's best, show the growing preoccupation, through the years of the depression and the New Deal, with social justice.

By 1936 Dos Passos had completed his trilogy, and our fiction of the thirties had revealed its chief change in pattern from that of the twenties. A parallel change could be noted in our drama, as typified by the early work of Eugene O'Neill and the early work of Clifford Odets. O'Neill's first plays—and in many ways his most impressive—were concerned with the disinherited, against the background of the sea, the slum, the unproductive farm. Odets' first plays were also concerned with the disinherited, but not as isolated beaten individuals, rather as part of the great mass of society, inchoate yet rising against social injustice.

The thirties seem in retrospect a more coherent if more limited period of expression than the twenties. And the forties? It comes as a shock to realize that they are nearly at an end, for they have witnessed no few figures with anything like the weight of production of any of the leading novelists of the thirties. There has also been much less production by the novelists already known. Dos Passos has not written an important novel for a dozen years. Hemingway has not yet written any novel since *For Whom the Bell Tolls* in 1940. Faulkner, Farrell, Steinbeck have hardly increased their range since then.

What are the reasons for this break? The big and obvious one is the war, and yet when we recall the First World War, the situation was very different. Many writers were emerging just before 1914, some of them too old for military service and so continuing to write through 1918, and others began to emerge at the war's end. One heavily altered factor is the length of time during which America was involved in the recent war. Yet even before then, by the end of the thirties, there began to be a collapse of the novel of social protest, not because the issues were not still grave, but because they had become so much graver, so much harder to handle.

In a time increasingly flooded with rival propagandas, we have come to a still greater awareness of the distance between the official and the actual. In the years just before, and now after the war, there has been a special importance in the little magazine for the experimental writer who found that what he had to say did not fit into the mode of the slick magazines, and who needed to strike out anew. What he had to say did not fit into the conventional mode because it was often agonizing. It was often an acute conflict between the outer and the inner, which came to expression not in a sustained form but in a short story.

Some deep awareness of that conflict also formed the common denominator between the older writers who have impressed our most recent beginners in fiction. The vogue, especially among readers under thirty, of authors of such diverse value as Henry James and Kafka, Henry Miller and Anais Nin, bespeaks their common concern with escape, not from the real, but from the monstrously unreal.

Some of the most recent short story writers from the

little magazines are now beginning to appear in volume form, most notably J. F. Powers and Peter Taylor. But their work, though excellent in quality, is still a little too limited to support generalizations. More certain comparisons may be based upon the work of the best-known writer for the theatre to have appeared in the forties. The plays of Tennessee Williams reveal the decade's particular awareness of the tensions between the inner and the outer life. Like O'Neill and Odets, he too is engaged with the disinherited, but his portrayal of them is characteristically of the case histories of fevered sufferers driven in upon themselves or escaping only in fantasy.

In mentioning the names of the newest writers, one must be even more conscious of the tentativeness of his judgments, especially since the work of the war generation, the generation of John Burns and Norman Mailer, is still mainly ahead. But whatever the case may prove to be in the fifties, the forties have been a time when it was hard for the writer to possess enough steadiness or enough coherence for creative renewal.

The great exception has been in our poetry, the domain in which there has always been the deepest consciousness of the need to resist all official versions. The emergence of Karl Shapiro and Robert Lowell, to name only the two most clearly outstanding talents, is a reminder that in the thirties most of the new names had been in fiction or drama. In poetry, though there had been exceptional first books by, for example, Robert Penn Warren and Delmore

Schwartz, there had been no American group to put beside that of Auden and Spender, who had emerged in England in the early thirties. This is again a very different situation from that prevailing in the twenties when many new American poets were flourishing. And as we look back now, from our mid-century, the most remarkable single feature of our twentieth-century literature is, I believe, the abundance and variety of our poetry. There have been more poets of real quality than during any previous period of American history. More than that, for the first time American poetry seems to be comparable to that written in any European country within the same span. In establishing the contrast between the official and the actual, I take our poetry to be the single most important piece of evidence.

The familiar and convenient, if not altogether accurate, date for the beginning of this poetic renaissance is October 1912, with the first issue, in Chicago, of *Poetry: A Magazine of Verse.* The early issues of that magazine now read like an anthology of most of our best-known poets, remarkably different from one another, and from widely separate parts of the country. One of its first discoveries was Vachel Lindsay's "General William Booth Enters into Heaven," the title poem of a volume in 1913. In 1914 he followed that up with *The Congo,* and that year was also marked by Robert Frost's first volume to gain recognition in America, *North of Boston, A Boy's Will* having been published in England the year before. In 1914 there had also appeared Amy Lowell's first distinctive work, *Sword*

Blades and Poppy Seed, and she had become the most vocal spokesman for "the new poetry." In 1915 came Edgar Lee Masters' *Spoon River Anthology,* and in 1916 Carl Sandburg's *Chicago Poems* and Edwin Arlington Robinson's most distinguished achievement, *The Man Against the Sky.*

Robinson had, of course, issued his first book to a small audience almost twenty years before that, but since Whitman's death in 1892, Robinson and William Vaughn Moody had been the only two poets to attempt anything like a major note. Furthermore, if you look back in trying to account for this poetic flowering, you realize that all the years since the Civil War had yielded very little poetry, with the lonely exceptions of Emily Dickinson in New England and Sidney Lanier in the South. Why then, near the opening of the second decade of the twentieth century, this sudden and abundant flowering? What can it tell us about our American civilization and some of its aims and aspirations?

It is interesting, for one thing, to notice the age of these new voices at the time of their first distinctive books. Lindsay was thirty-four, Frost and Sandburg were both thirty-eight, Amy Lowell was forty, Masters was forty-six. That is not young for poets. This fact suggests something long in preparation which only finally found an audience —writers coming out of great isolation and then responding to the quickening stimulus of discovering themselves no longer alone.

But why just then? It was doubtless owing in part to

the background of an age of protest, as represented by the work of the muckrakers, an age of protest which was also an age of hope, of reform, of untried possibilities. It was a period of new openings in the other arts as well, as our painters responded to postimpressionist European painting in the great Armory show of 1913. Our producers and actors were beginning to build up a Little Theatre movement, which provided both a theatre and an audience for the first plays of O'Neill. America was growing aware of its new architecture in the skyscrapers, of the potentialities in its new jazz music. It was a time of promise in the air when "the fiddles were tuning." There was the feeling that a rich harvest was about to ripen, just as there had been during the first phase of our American renaissance, in the age of Emerson and Melville.

Three years earlier than Harriet Monroe's magazine, the man who was to contribute its London Letter, Ezra Pound, had already published his *Personae*. T. S. Eliot's first poem, "The Love Song of J. Alfred Prufrock," was printed in *Poetry* on Pound's recommendation, in 1915. By then several other younger poets had begun to appear at various American colleges. Edna Millay's first book, *Renascence,* came out in 1917, shortly after she left Vassar. E. E. Cummings had graduated from Harvard in 1915, Archibald MacLeish from Yale in the same year, just before Stephen Benét was a freshman.

The most significant fact is that from then until now there has been a greater continuity in our poetry as a whole than in our prose, not merely through the accident that more of the older generation of our poets are still alive, but primarily because, undistracted by the demands of publisher and publicity, the poets have persevered in their devotion to their craft. For example, how increasingly solid now are the reputations of Frost and Eliot, to pick two poets as unlike as possible. When the history of the poetry in our time is written, I believe that these two will be the pivotal figures, dividing, through their contrasts, much of the ground between them. The superficial contrasts are those between the plain man and the Harvard intellectual, between the native New Englander and the expatriate Englishman. The more important contrasts are between the poet of the country and the poet of the city, of man in nature as against man in our increasingly metropolitan society; between the poet of individualism in the strain of Emerson and the poet of the weakness of individualism in the strain of Hawthorne and James; between the poet of sureness, leading at times to complacence, and the poet of doubt, leading to mystical brooding over issues that are hard to resolve.

There are many other ways of suggesting the range and vitality in the poetry of our age. Our poets might be divided into the descendants of Whitman and the descendants of Poe. Sandburg would then be a central figure in one line, whereas those whose inheritance from Poe stems through French symbolism would make up the other. Hart Crane, the most gifted new poet in the twenties, attempted to span the two lines, using in *The Bridge* the technique of *The Waste Land* to reaffirm something of the vision of Whitman and Melville. But Crane, the sensitive register of some of the fiercest tensions in our culture, was caught, despite his intense desire to celebrate America, in Poe's "unmerciful disaster," and became one of the most suffering witnesses to modern rootlessness.

Another index to the variety of our poetry lies in the fact that nearly every region, not merely the East and the Middle West, has found some expression through it. One of the most striking features of American literature since 1920—and not in poetry alone—is the amount of talent coming from the South, or rather, from many various sections of the South, because the South of Faulkner is very different from the South of Wolfe, and both these Souths are distinct from that of the poets who grouped around John Crowe Ransom and Allen Tate at Nashville. Their distinction in phrasing, their urbanity and irony, suggest some of the qualities that Eliot had also been bringing back into vogue. But Ransom developed his style independently of Eliot, and made his own kind of witty poetry in a language both colloquial and deliberately archaic. The reason for this mixture, which is the main reason also for his irony, is his desire to suggest the difficulty and yet the value of maintaining whatever cultural continuities we can in our ever changing society, in our age of bare science and brute fact.

The brutalities of the age are the pervading theme of another poet two thousand miles away in point of view no less than in region. The California which Robinson Jeffers has evoked is very somber. His gravely eloquent lyrics are possessed by the thought that we have reached the continent's end, with no further frontier ahead, and with the softly corrupt values of Hollywood invading what hardly a life span ago was still a desert coast. He is also possessed by a cyclical theory of history, by the thought that we are going down the dark mountains to destruction.

Poets are, to be sure, not finally judged according to their regions, and a more valuable kind of category lies in the reputations which are now rising among the younger practitioners in their craft. For the poets under thirty are the makers of the taste of today and tomorrow, and if you talk with them you will find, among their most frequent admirations, Wallace Stevens and Marianne Moore. These two expert craftsmen also have in common the fact that both have taken the nature and function of art itself for one of their chief themes. Stevens, whose first published poem appeared in *Poetry* in 1914, but whose first book, *Harmonium,* did not appear until nearly a decade later, when he was forty-four, has proved during the last decade to be the kind of artist of whom we have not had nearly enough examples in America, the artist who is far more prolific in his sixties than in his twenties. The younger poets now regard him as the most resourceful master of their art now writing in America, as one who has assimilated and made his own some of the riches of continental writing, some of the brilliance and color and suavity that we associate particularly with French poetry.

All I have wanted to suggest by this series of partial groupings is the impossibility in such diversity of any single or simple assessment. Karl Shapiro, discussing our poetry and its issues in the *Essay on Rime* which he wrote during his years in the army, has suggested much the same thing. Only Shapiro, as befits a serious younger artist, was more preoccupied with shortcomings than with successes. He dwelt on some of the confusions rife in the art of our time, confusions in prosody, confusions in language, confusions in belief. In his own work he is much concerned with the renewal of a more popular poetry. Yet when he turns to Whitman, he is aware of the necessity not to swallow Whitman whole. He has remarked that the word "America" is "the chief enemy of modern poetry." He means that the wide, loose generalization is no longer helpful to us. For the living sources of poetry, the poet must hew closely again to concrete objects, he must portray the given person, place, and thing that he knows.

Robert Lowell—to sketch in a little more where our poetry finds itself now and thus bring my description of it to a conclusion—stems rather from Eliot and the metaphysicals and symbolists. He has made a further reversal of his Puritan New England background than is to be found in Eliot. He has gone beyond the Anglican tradition to the Roman, beyond Donne and Marvell to Catholic poets of a more flamboyant imagery.

The work of both Shapiro and Lowell may be represented by elegies. The striking accomplishment in Shapiro's "Elegy for a Dead Soldier" is the thoroughly honest portrait which the poet, the detached intellectual who has yet known service as a sergeant in the medical corps in the Pacific, manages to give of the ordinary GI in his animation and confidence, in his ignorance and cynicism and his most staggering limitation:

> He hated other races, south or east
> And shoved them to the margin of his mind.

With unobtrusive eloquence this poem discloses the tension between the good and bad qualities in our national character. The soldier's blank incomprehension:

> To him the red flag marked the sewer main,

is balanced against his sure possession:

> Doors opened, and he recognized no class.

And the incipient brutality of how he could

> Take interest in a gang-war like a game,

is held in some check by his natural warmth:

> His laugh was real, his manners were home made.

In this mixed stuff of common experience, Shapiro is saying, we Americans must struggle for whatever humane values we are to possess—and articulate.

What Lowell has to convey is far more somber. He was a conscientious objector who went to prison for his convictions, but his elegy, "The Quaker Graveyard at Nantucket," is also an elegy for a casualty of the war, for one of his cousins drowned in naval service. It is not, like Shapiro's poem, a character portrayal, but a poem of the sea. Lowell's daring and violent images have an intensity which no other young poet has attempted since Hart Crane's death, and his evocations of Captain Ahab and the *Pequod* stand firm even in comparison with Melville's splendor.

In his spiritual meditations, Lowell, of course, searches beyond the Quakers, just as he does in another poem about earlier New England, called "Children of Light." That title is ironic, for where the Puritans found their enkindling truth, Lowell sees only blinding darkness. If Shapiro senses the great odds we fight against in the unpreparedness of our national character to play a just international role, Lowell has apparently rejected our present society as hopelessly lost. His recurrent symbols are those of degradation and decay. In "The Dead in Europe" and "The Exile's Return" he dwells on the incalculable wreckage our age has wrought. In his Boston poems he evokes a city burning itself out in heavy corruption.

In poems like those of Shapiro and Lowell we reach the most essential elements in our recent thought and feeling, so far as these have come to literary expression. This statement assumes—as I have been assuming throughout—that if we are to find a pattern in literature, we must reckon with both the immediate and the enduring. That is often very difficult to do. To point up what I have in mind, there is Henry James's observation that two books dealing with serfdom, *A Sportsman's Sketches* and *Uncle*

Tom's Cabin, both appeared in 1852. James goes on to say that in Turgenev's book

> No single episode pleads conclusively against the peculiar institution of Russia; the lesson is the cumulative testimony of a multitude of fine touches—in an after-sense of sadness that sets wise readers thinking. It would be difficult to name a work that contains better instruction for those heated spirits who are fond of taking sides on the question of "art for art." It offers a capital example of moral meaning giving a sense of form and form giving relief to moral meaning.

The Grapes of Wrath and *Pale Horse, Pale Rider* both appeared in 1939. There is no comparison between the importance of Steinbeck's subject and that of Katherine Anne Porter. Steinbeck's is one of the major themes of the depression: the uprooting of the Oklahoma sharecroppers during the time of the dust storms, and their trek across to California to swell the army of the other dispossessed seasonal workers. Miss Porter's title story deals with a girl's loss of her lover in the flu epidemic at the end of the First World War. But through her "multitude of fine touches," Miss Porter recaptures the very atmosphere of that moment of crisis in our history, its feeling of release and promise for some, of loss and desolation for others.

Steinbeck's pages already seem hastily thrown together, many of his images broad but inexact, the conversations of his Okies factitious in their folksiness. The more exacting skills of Miss Porter, who has been writing very sparingly since the twenties, will prove to have conveyed a more persuasive "moral meaning" through her picture of what she has called "that true and human world of which the artist is a living part." This comparison is not meant to underrate the value of Steinbeck's vigorous propaganda, but to suggest that an enduring work must have a less hurried command of its material, a more organic interplay between content and form.

We need to hold fast to that proposition if we are to find the real pattern in our literature, to perceive what it has been and not what we wish it might have been. What we find will often be disturbing. Consider the poet and the novelist who have had the most influence in America during the past quarter of a century, measuring influence in the most vital way, in the effect they have had upon younger writers. The peculiar role that is often played by literature could hardly be realized more sharply than through the fact that Eliot and Hemingway, who do not correspond at any points to what Dos Passos has called "our story-book democracy," have given to a whole generation of readers by now the sense of life that comes through expert expression.

The implications for our society may be very grave when our most gifted writer of prose is so possessed by themes of destruction and death, and when the leading poet now, since Yeats's death, in the English language, so often envisages our time as being on the verge of new dark ages. Both Hemingway and Eliot are deeply disturbing in the very way that neither Hollywood, nor the slick magazines, nor the National Association of the Manufacturers of the American Way of Life would have any writers be. But disturbance is the unfailing sign that the rigidity of death has not set in; and the disturbance provided by the real artist, unlike that of the sensationalist, comes from his having patiently perfected his control over his words until they can embody, not what he would, but what he has to say.

The effect of such articulation upon the beginning writer is not to depress him, no matter how one-sided or limited the vision of life of the master writer to whom he is attracted. The effect of perfection in art is to stimulate the young writer to devise expert expression for his own very different sense of life, to the very degree that it does not correspond to the experience of an Eliot or a Hemingway. This is the awakening function of art ignored by the official psychologies. It was not ignored by Marx or Engels who so admired Balzac despite his monarchic and Catholic views. For they recognized that the responsibility of the artist is not to solve in advance the tensions of the society he lives in, but simply—yet this is a task for a lifetime—to render, to the full, existence as he has known it to be. The role of a Hemingway or an Eliot, though scarcely that of a Balzac or a Dante, is to keep alive the vital, delicate, and always menaced accuracy of communication, without which there can be no renewed discovery of man by man.

We have come now to the heart of the difference between the official and the actual, and are perhaps finally in a position to generalize about some of the permanent rather than the transient qualities of American literature. Whether we turn to our poets who are read by a relatively small public, and yet in whom the future will find the most searching image of our time; or whether we return to the writers with whom we started, our naturalistic writers of fiction with the widest international vogue, we will find the same fact: the essentially critical nature of American literature.

One of the most long-standing and robust of our traditions, from Benjamin Franklin and Mark Twain, is the healthy value of an unimpeded flow of satire—gay, embullient, stinging, or savage, as the situation may require. To lose touch with that tradition now when there are so many balloons to be deflated, so many enormities to be mocked out of existence, would be to yield the remaining vestiges of our integrity into the ready hands of the blurb writers. Among the best instances of the vitality of satire is that provided by the earlier works of Sinclair Lewis. Note what a firmness *Babbitt* in particular still has, a firmness which is lacking in Lewis' later books where his aims became less sharp and certain. Furthermore, out-and-out propaganda tracts, like those of Upton Sinclair or Howard Fast, however crude in form, have often served to clear the heavy air. It is especially necessary to stress that fact, since Sinclair's works were used by the Nazis to demonstrate the corruptions of American society. At that point many of our sentimental nationalists took the position that by castigating the shortcomings in our culture, our intellectuals had become irresponsible. But criticism is a risk that must always be run by a society that is not afraid of itself. The only adequate defense against it is to prove that it is one-sided or untrue, and the only way to render it invalid is to remedy the abuses that have been attacked, not to pretend that they do not exist.

Yet we must also remember that our literature is not merely one of protest, but of affirmation. The most eloquent passage in Dos Passos' *U.S.A.* is the one beginning, "They have clubbed us off the streets," where for once the vague estheticism of his "camera eye" became charged with a social affirmation as he gave his uncompromising denunciation of the murderers of Sacco and Vanzetti. In the moment of remembering that passage, we realize what an appalling light is thrown upon our recent society by the fact that injustice done to two men twenty years ago could then stir people throughout the world, which has since been drenched with the blood of injustice done to millions. That overwhelming fact has much bearing upon the general collapse of the novel of social conviction at the end of the thirties, though the objective need for a people's democracy becomes ever more urgent.

The need for comprehending and humane writers to understand and interpret our society has also become more urgent in the forties, for the very reasons that have made it more difficult for such writers to find their directions. A central function of literary tradition lies in the power of our great books to steady and sustain us, to help us realize again the values that keep us alive. Out of all the books by the recent authors I have mentioned, the one that might best perform that function now is Sherwood Anderson's *Winesburg, Ohio*. Probing beneath the flat, starved surfaces of the small town that Lewis caricatured so effectively, Anderson found the still unspent sources of love. One of his characters, reflecting on the bitter fact that "men coming out of Europe and given millions of square miles of black, fertile land, mines, and forests, have failed in the challenge given them by fate and have produced out of the stately order of nature only the sordid disorder of man," cried out: "There is a curse on my country. Everyone has come here for gain, to grow rich, to achieve. Suppose they should begin to want to live here?" Facing that question, Anderson set himself, like his own Windy McPherson's son, to the task of "understanding those other lives in love." He wanted to awaken his readers to "the thing beyond words, beyond passion—the fellowship in living, the fellowship in life."

That seems immeasurably harder now than in the mood of promise in which Anderson shared at the end of the First World War. Such a mood cannot be evoked at will or without rededication to the extension of economic and social democracy at home and abroad. But such a rededication is essential if our writers are to escape from their pervasive sense of alienation, if their worlds are not to remain private, if they are to repossess, as Anderson did, the central core in Whitman's meaning—his unshakable belief in solidarity with the common life.

Chapter III

Science and Humanity

Detlev W. Bronk

I T IS appropriate that one of the chapters of this series should be devoted to science, for science is responsible for much of the present structure of American civilization. It is appropriate too that science should be included in a series of lectures dedicated to Benjamin Franklin, for he has a continuing influence on contemporary American science. He was the first American scientist, in the modern sense of the word, with a modern attitude toward the personal and the social values of science.

It was natural that Franklin, who was also a man of affairs, should cultivate science as a means of changing the world in which he lived. The world is certainly changed, but the reasons why scientists do the things they do are not very different from Franklin's.

The most familiar of Franklin's motives was his interest in the practical values of science. Then, as before and now, men lived under the threat of destruction by natural forces. Plagues were enemies made doubly dangerous because the attacking forces were still unseen through the eyes of science. The unpredicted natural

58

elements were fearsome hazards to be faced whenever
men voyaged upon the seas. Starvation stalked its human
prey and made men slaves to unremitting labor. Against
such threats of destruction science was man's most powerful weapon—a weapon recognized by Franklin when he
created the American Philosophical Society in Philadelphia "For the Promotion of Useful Knowledge."

If we are to comprehend the role of science in American
civilization, we must look beyond the scientist's desire
for practical accomplishments. It is especially important
that we do so at a time when every man's life is profoundly
affected by the scientist's actions and at a time when the
national government has assumed a direct responsibility
for training scientists with tax-contributed money. It is
desirable to explain scientists when they are being her-
alded as mystical supermen or as evil denizens of an
ivory tower.

Throughout Franklin's letters there are passages such
as this which emphasize curiosity as an incentive to scientific research: "I would beg leave to recommend to the
curious in this branch of natural philosophy that they
repeat, with care and accurate observation, the experiments I have reported." Franklin's interest in science as
a mere means of satisfying his curiosity about the nature
of things is less familiar, but was no less potent than his
interest in its practical usefulness. Few may doubt that
curiosity is the most powerful motive in science, because
it is common to all men; it may seem unnecessary to com-

ment further. I do so because, even in this age of science, curiosity is often considered a bothersome trait which has got us into a great deal of trouble from the days of the Garden of Eden to those of Hiroshima.

There is opposition to curiosity first in childhood. Only the most patient parent encourages its free development at the expense of his personal peace. Only the wisest of teachers discard the easy methods of didactic instruction to follow as counselors at the heels of students who freely satisfy their curiosity. Even in the scientific laboratory the student's curiosity is suppressed and the laboratory becomes a training ground for technical manipulation rather than a place for intellectual exploration. The present tendency to create an educational system which thus suppresses curiosity for the sake of "efficient" education robs modern civilization of the true scientists it needs.

Nor will the scientists' research flourish unless they have freedom to follow their curiosity. Against this there is now strong opposition. When science seemed rather unimportant, scientists were left pretty much alone to do as they wished—provided they were able to live. Nowadays science is recognized as necessary for human welfare and national survival. Because of this there are many who are willing to support science provided they can organize and direct the scientists' activities—about which they know but little. And there are those who believe that the usefulness of scientific research can be increased and its practical yield multiplied by putting many scientists to work under the controlled direction of a few.

There are problems and there are times which require that the individual freedom of the scientist be submerged in a common effort for the public good. But there is a grave danger that the present demand by publicists, industrialists, and public administrators for large-scale scientific organizations may impede progress.

The most important discoveries of scientific research have come from the intellectual adventures of individual scientists. No one directed Newton to discover the laws of gravitation. No one organized Faraday's discoveries in electricity for the benefit of the modern electrical age. No one suggested to Roentgen that he discover x-rays for the diagnosis of human ills. No one instructed Niels Bohr to pave the way for atomic energy. Great scientific discoveries will usually elude direction and organization as surely as would the creation of great music or poetry, or sculpture or art. Much of scientific research is exploration of the unknown and I, for one, do not believe it is possible to direct the course of an explorer through unexplored territory.

Scientists have a second purpose, no weaker than curiosity, but more difficult to achieve. It is the desire to bring order out of chaos. Curiosity drives the scientist to seek new facts through observation and experiment. The wish to relate those facts and fit them into a consistent pattern is the motive which causes him to formulate natural laws, and the concepts which make scientific facts meaningful and usable.

The achievement of such order in the observations of

nature is an acute intellectual satisfaction. Those who suddenly grasp the relation of previously unrelated facts, and thus see their relevance, experience a deep esthetic satisfaction. It is in that phase of scientific endeavor that facts and observations are formed into the structure of knowledge, which is the foundation for further discoveries. This is the role of the scientist's creative imagination. Without freedom and leisure for the play of his imagination, a scientist becomes only a fact-gatherer, dealing with the bare bones of science, unarticulated and unclothed with the flesh of meaning.

This subtle process, from which so much of human value comes, has been described with rare insight by John Livingston Lowes in *The Road to Xanadu.** In that study of the ways of poetic creation there are these passages:

"The ways of the creative process are not the monopoly of poetry. In the field of science, too, the imagination draws the immense confusion of phenomena within the unfolding conception of an ordered universe.

"For years, through intense and unremitting observation, Darwin had been accumulating masses of facts which pointed to a momentous conclusion. But they pointed through a maze of baffling inconsistencies. Then, all at once a flash of vision came. Only then, and not before, could he slowly frame the great statement of the theory of evolution" which has reshaped men's thoughts.

* Published by Houghton Mifflin Company. Copyright, 1927, by John Livingston Lowes.

And, in considering the work of Newton, Lowes goes on to say: "The leap of the imagination from the fall of an apple in the garden at Woolsthorpe to an architectonic conception, cosmic in its scope and grandeur, is one of the dramatic moments in the history of human thought. But in that pregnant moment there flashed together the profound and daring observations and conjectures of a long period of years; upon the instant of illumination followed other years of rigorous and protracted labor, before the *Principia* appeared," forever to change our relations with the world in which we live.

Thus to bring order out of chaos and attain understanding is one of the great purposes of science, for which a scientist will gladly spend his life. As we plan our new age of science we shall do well to preserve an environment in which this purpose will be nurtured, despite the urgency of present needs. For it is unlikely that the scientists' imagination will often leap to a specified goal. A chaos of facts will seldom fall into an ordered, predetermined pattern, useful for a certain end.

I fear I may not have chosen wisely in selecting Darwin and Newton as examples of the contemporary American scientist. Those who think of scientific research as an organized effort to gain material benefits will say that they are rare instances of scientific genius. Ordinary men, they may add, work differently, and best achieve their scientific functions through organization and direction by a master mind. With this I cannot agree. Creative imagination is not an esoteric faculty, unique to genius. It is characteristic of all creative endeavor, through which the human mind discovers order in a chaotic world.

Modern scientific endeavor must certainly be organized to provide the instruments for research and the combination of human skills necessary for diverse experimental tasks. But society will gain most from scientists if they are given freedom to observe, to experiment and think. Science is playing an important role in America's world-wide struggle for the freedom of the individual. In order that science may play that role well, the freedom of the scientists must be preserved against the regimentation of over-stuffed organizations here at home. Despite the fantasies of scientific planners in and out of Russia, I should be surer of the social value of a mere score of scientists who are free to investigate and explain the facts of nature than of a thousand who are organized for the solution of a directed end.

In a democracy, however, it is not easy to justify such personal leisure and freedom, when most of the population must labor at routine tasks. "Why," asked a member of a Congressional appropriations committee recently, "should so few be supported to learn so much when so many know so little?" It is well to admit to such skeptics that some of the most important contributions of science to human welfare have no obvious practical usefulness. But let them consider how in a few generations we have been freed from the fear of natural forces that were mysterious and malevolent; how we have been freed from slavery to ignorance and superstition. At a time when science is prized for its contributions of instruments and weapons, of food and health and physical power and comfort, I would remind you that the pleasure which comes from an understanding of the beauties and forces of nature is a subtle value of science which extends the horizons of our intellect and enriches our lives.

Scientists are largely to blame for the fact that these intangible rewards of scientific investigation are not generally understood. One never hears musicians or sculptors or poets justify their role in society with the claim that they increase the physical well-being of their fellow men. Society values them, insofar as it values them at all, for the pleasure they give to life. Scientists, however, emphasize the material benefits of science because they are readily comprehended and accepted. In doing so, they misrepresent and belittle some of their major contributions to human welfare. Scientific research is one of the great adventures of the human mind. When the spirit of that adventure is understood, it will quicken the life and raise the hopes of people everywhere.

This is sufficient justification for the support of science as a major activity in society. But the effects of science do not end there. New ideas inevitably lead to new patterns of life. The discovery of natural knowledge, no matter how remote from human affairs it may seem, ultimately affects the actions as well as the thoughts of men. Scientific knowledge of the nature of the sun and the elements has displaced them from their role as gods and has saved the lives of multitudes who would have been sacrificed to placate the gods' supposed demands.

Such intellectual and spiritual effects of science are, in part, responsible for the changing patterns of culture; so also are the practical results of science. This is especially true of American culture, which has been profoundly influenced by machines and the products of machines.

There is scarcely an aspect of American civilization which has not been shaped by scientific research and the applications of research. Our supply of materials comes from the laboratory as well as from nature. Industry depends upon power, scientifically created and controlled. Commerce requires swift transportation. Men live in cities heated and lighted and kept sanitary by scientific methods. Accordingly, the maintenance of American society requires a great army of scientifically trained men and women.

The characteristics of a continually developing American civilization are such that there is also an ever-increasing need for scientific investigation. The discovery of new metals makes possible the design of new machines, but that may require the development of new mathematical procedures. Atomic energy has created new elements which have made possible the discovery of new treatments for disease. In turn, such treatments require new methods for human protection against radiation. Each new scientific development creates further problems which require more study and research.

The demands for the fruits of science are further aug-
mented by the recent war and by the present international
hazards. This is an old story in the modern tempo, for
the practical importance of science to warfare has been
long recognized. Galileo and Leonardo were employed by
their governments to improve artillery and the art of
fortification. From that time onward, science has shaped
the pattern of warfare until today science is recognized as
one of the first lines of national defense. Scientists are
required by the thousands for the training and operation
of our armed forces. New weapons of aggression, forged
by science, require of scientists new means for counter-
action and defense.

Our culture, shaped by science and dependent upon
science for its preservation, is now changing the pattern
and status of science in America. Of that new status there
are four aspects worthy of consideration.

The first is a great increase in the financial support of
research. During the year 1930, 166 million dollars were
expended for scientific investigation and for its development towards practical purposes. By the year 1947 this
amount had been increased to more than one billion
dollars, which does not include expenditures in the field
of atomic energy. Looking into the future, the President's
Scientific Research Board has recommended that the
amount should be two and a quarter billion dollars by
1957.

It is significant to recite additional figures. In 1930 the
United States Government expended 23 millions for sci-

ence, or 14 per cent of the total. In 1947 the federal sum was 625 millions, an increase of thirty-fold which is now more than 50 per cent of the total national expenditure for scientific research. Obviously, those who are responsible for the determination of our national policies believe that the support of science is a governmental function.

But it is not surprising that the sudden inclusion of science as a major part of the framework of government should meet strong opposition. On the one hand, the federal support of science is opposed because of fear that science and scientists will be deprived of their freedom, and that the fruits of science will wither. On the other hand, it is feared that the central government may gain from its vassal scientists too much power over the American people. To shrink from such dangers is to doubt the virtues of American democracy.

If there be any field of activity which is the proper province of the national government, it is the encouragement of research. It is from scientific research that our citizens have the greatest promise of higher standards of living, better health, and security against the dangers of foreign aggression. Individuals, unaided, cannot reap the full benefits of science.

After a war in which we have been forced to destroy vast quantities of our natural resources, it is well to give thought to the future sources of our national strength. Also, it is well to consider the sources of that which we must contribute to rebuild a war-devastated world. Fortunately, our greatest national resource is one that need have no limits. I refer to our knowledge of the physical universe, our knowledge of plant and animal life, our knowledge of the workings of our own bodies in health and disease.

It would be unfortunate if the full responsibility for the support of science were relegated to the government. The integration of science into American culture requires that many individuals have the status of participating stockholders in the advancement of science. That this is increasingly so is a healthy characteristic of our social customs. University departments of teaching and research are supported by great numbers of individuals who are conscious of their responsible part in society. Countless industries are this year expending half a billion dollars on the discovery and development of new knowledge. Foundations for the furtherance of research now receive the benefactions of millions who, to the limits of their resources, follow the generous example of the wealthy few. Such are the National Foundation for Infantile Paralysis and the American Cancer Society. I would add that more than money is derived from this widespread but untaxed participation. Participants gain some understanding of the meaning of science; they develop a better appreciation of the values of science. Thus our citizens become better qualified to control the scientific policies of the nation.

The wise use of these increased financial resources requires a great increase in the number of scientists. This is the second characteristic of the new status of science.

It is not long since scientific research was the leisure

avocation of teachers and laymen or the exclusive occupation of but a few isolated workers. Today universities, industries, and the government compete to fill unfilled needs for many thousands of scientific investigators. The number of scientists, technicians, and engineers has increased only one-tenth as fast since 1940 as has the expenditure for research and development. While the budget was increasing 335 per cent, the supply of trained man power expanded only 35 per cent.

The technological and scientific progress of the nation and its operation depends upon less than one-half of one per cent of our population; one-tenth of one per cent of our population are actually engaged in scientific research and development; less than twenty-five thousand among our population of 150 million have had the advanced training for scientific research and teaching represented by the doctorate.

To meet these needs, the universities are straining every available facility. Private and public foundations and industries are contributing large sums for the education of scientists, and the government is initiating fellowship programs for the training of young men and women. The Atomic Energy Commission alone has appropriated two and one-half million dollars for such fellowships during the coming year or two. This is the development of a national resource of great importance.

As we go forward with scientific education on a grand scale, I would suggest that we paraphrase the old adage: "You can lead a horse to water, but you can't make him

drink"—you can train scientists and lead them to a laboratory but you can't make them discover the facts of nature.
It is for this reason that I have discussed the motives or
the characteristics of a scientist. Unless a man or a woman
be fired by curiosity and possess the patience to investigate nature, he will not add to scientific knowledge and
human welfare.

No individual is endowed with all the qualities required for the pursuit of science, but there are vast, un-
touched reservoirs of human talent. For the advancement
of science, as for the advancement of every phase of our
civilization, we must learn to identify and to train those
who are best qualified for a given social function, without
regard for family fortune. Only thus are we likely to
meet the specialized needs of a complex culture.

For several centuries the universities have been the
nurseries and the homes of science. Now, as the number
of scientists trained in the universities increases, more and
more of the scientists migrate elsewhere.

The university began to lose its place as the only home
of research about 1900, when the laboratories of the General Electric Company and of the Bell Telephone system
were first established. Such industrial laboratories have
grown and multiplied without a stop in sight, and now
they have their numerous federal counterparts. This
spread of science outside the universities is a third characteristic of its modern pattern.

It is well for the universities that this is so. If they were
to assume the responsibility for all that can and must be

done by science, they would prostitute their proper functions. A university is the ideal environment for thought and investigation and the spread of knowledge. The application of that knowledge to the practical problems of today is the function of other institutions which are being created for that purpose. The university scientists who withstand the pressure to solve practical problems of the present are the scientists who are free to pave the way for useful applications of the future.

Many of those who are devoted to the discovery of new knowledge have developed a concern for its social effects. I would name this uneasy sense of responsibility as a fourth characteristic of modern American science. It is natural that this should be so in troubled times of great change, for which science is in no small part the cause.

The critical needs for national survival marshaled our science to an extraordinary degree during this recent war. But the scientists' satisfaction in their achievements, which armed human courage, has been sobered by the realization that new forces of destruction were thus unleashed. Nor has the end of conflict been reassuring. The accomplishments of ages lie in ruins, and the hardly gained knowledge of nature is used by both, in the conflict between the good and the evil.

Science itself is neither good nor evil. It is "neither a benign nor a malignant activity of man." Science is a quest for knowledge and understanding, to be applied for human use as men desire. It is with such thoughts in mind that scientists feel an increasing obligation to participate in decisions as to how their discoveries and technical developments shall be used. But the fulfillment of this obligation will require scientists to acquire a knowledge of human affairs and of the motives which shape public policy. Even then scientists will most effectively participate in the wise use of science in public affairs by disseminating an understanding of science to those in public authority and to those who shape popular opinion.

Certainly it is desirable in a democracy that every citizen take an active part in the direction of government, to the limits of his abilities. Accordingly the growing social conscience of scientists is desirable. So, too, is the slowly increasing participation of scientists in the affairs of government. But our complex social structure requires that each citizen have a primary responsibility for some special task. Thus I return to the point that our future welfare requires that a goodly number of scientists be free to study nature without regard for the practical needs of the moment.

The encouragement of scientific exploration or research —in contrast with the application of science—has not always been a characteristic of American culture. Commenting upon this a century ago, Alexis de Tocqueville attributed the emphasis upon immediate, practical values to the traits of a democracy, where, said he, "men . . . seldom indulge in meditation . . . and require nothing of science but its special applications to the useful arts and the means of rendering life comfortable." The observations of this distinguished observer of democracy in America were not far wrong, for fundamental research has flourished less here than in Europe. But his assumptions as to the reason for our emphasis on the practical aspects of science have been disproved by the recent development of basic science within our democracy. There are significant causes for this increased emphasis on fundamental research.

One of these causes is the spread of college education and the inclusion of science in the academic curriculum. To this I would add adult education in science by the radio and by scientific journalism which has reached high standards here in the United States. But as President Conant has emphasized in his book *On Understanding Science,* much of our education still deals with the results of science; there is little discussion of the methods and sequence of science. Until this defect is corrected we face a popular demand that scientists mortgage their future usefulness by concentrating their efforts on the practical application of past discoveries.

Despite the inadequacies of scientific education for the layman, many recognize that Michael Faraday's discovery of electro-magnetic induction was necessary for the subsequent development of electric power and light and traction; that the botanical research of Gregor Mendel in the garden of a monastery paved the way for increased production by modern agriculture; that the theories of Willard Gibbs laid the foundations for much of our chemical industry.

Realizing this dependence of the practical upon that which is at first impractical, many intelligent citizens have supported basic research in universities, whence the discoveries flow into the stream of knowledge. The universities have thus assumed responsibility for exploring the endless frontiers of the nation.

In a democracy, it is appropriate that this national service should have been initiated by individuals. It is desirable that they should continue to accept that obligation. But it is also a proper responsibility of the national government which previously has been charged with the development, and protection for the future, of basic natural resources such as forests, water power, soil, and fisheries. Basic research, in contrast to applied research and technology, is not unlike such resources, for it provides new scientific knowledge of future value for our national welfare. This is the reason for the support of university research by the Public Health Service and the armed forces and by the proposed National Science Foundation.

In accepting such a partnership with the federal government the universities have assumed an obligation to preserve the freedom of scientists to seek "new trails to knowledge." Despite the present vigor of science, many who determine public policies see the desirability of applying a new discovery in the development of materials, machines, or weapons, in the treatment of disease or in the improvement of agriculture. Few have the faith to support abstract research, in the exploration of the unknown, for the benefit of future generations.

"If the Americans had been alone in the world," said De Tocqueville, "with the freedom and knowledge acquired by their forefathers and with the passions which are their own, they would not have been slow to discover that progress cannot long be made in the application of the sciences without cultivating the theory of them." We are not alone in the world, but we now occupy a position of preëminent power in world science. In our present position is it appropriate that we should benefit from the discoveries of scientists in other nations without contributing in return some discoveries to their benefit?

There can be no consideration of modern American science without regard to the international status of America. Our position in the world and the condition of the world depend upon science. If you suspect me of exaggeration, I suggest that you recall the influence of the atomic bomb on world thought and action.

But before I proceed further I would remind you that known science has no national boundaries. The properties of inorganic matter and the behavior of living organisms are not affected by the limits of states. Natural phenomena, observed anywhere, must be fitted into a consistent pattern of universal validity. This is the basis for the world-wide unity of science.

The genesis of new ideas is catalyzed by the work and thought of others. Recognizing this, scientists have been among the first to realize the dependence of their work upon the efforts of those in other lands. Together with the traders for rare goods they have sought intellectual products and new discoveries wherever they were to be found. It is worthy of emphasis that this desire for international coöperation derives from no unique nobility of spirit, but comes, rather, from the simple realization of the personal advantages that derive from a free exchange of ideas. If scientists are better prepared for the acceptance of the principles of world unity, it is because they have longer realized the benefits that come from such coöperation.

No one understood the universal value of science better than the founder of our University, Benjamin Franklin. Nowhere did he express his international philosophy better than in this directive to the commanders of all armed ships acting by commission from the Congress of the United States at war with Great Britain, in 1779:

Gentlemen, [said he] a ship was fitted out from England before the commencement of this war to make discoveries in unknown seas under the conduct of that most celebrated Navigator and Discoverer Captain Cook. This is an undertaking truly laudable in itself, because the increase of geographical knowledge facilitates the communication between distant nations and the exchange of useful products and manufactures, extends the arts, and science of other kinds is increased to the benefit of mankind in general. This, then, is to recommend to you that should the said Ship fall into your hands, you would not consider her as an enemy, nor suffer any plunder to be made of the effects contained in her, nor obstruct her immediate return to England.

The necessities of total war have changed international policies, but the spirit of Franklin still dominates American science. In this period of reconstruction our scientists again roam the free world for ideas and knowledge, and gladly receive their foreign colleagues who are free to come.

Our statesmen, too, follow the example of Franklin, the first American statesman. Scientific missions to foreign capitals have been established for the exchange of information, and large sums have been allotted under the Fulbright Act for the interchange of scholars. Most significant, perhaps, is the role of the American government and American scientists in rebuilding the physical facilities for scientific research and teaching in foreign countries. Our nation is but one of the nations in a civilization that is based upon science. Lasting benefits of the unprecedented European Recovery Program will depend in large measure on the degree to which European science recovers its ability to meet the needs of a modern society.

Science increased in any free country will be "increased to the benefit of mankind in general." The observations of Galileo and Copernicus extended the intellectual horizons of no one national group; the discoveries of Faraday, the Englishman, have eased the labors of the citizens of many countries; a cure for disease discovered in Holland will be as beneficial to a sufferer in New York as it would be if it were made in Philadelphia. The future of American science and the welfare of the American people depend upon the rehabilitation of science throughout the world. Without such a scientific recovery, the civilization of other nations will become very different from the American culture.

Even now we delude ourselves when we talk of living in an age of science. The cultures of America and Western Europe are very different from those of other areas. If science expands in America without a corresponding development everywhere, there will be a further imbalance of cultures. There lies a grave danger to peace and stability.

The use of modern science gives a nation tremendous power and material advantages. Accordingly it is natural in these days of international tension that those countries in which the practical aspects of science are developed to a high degree should be feared and suspected, and envied for the benefits they reap. This leads me to inject a comparison of American and Russian science. Excepting a few isolated, practical developments which would surely be used against us by an enemy, the discoveries of American scientists are free for all to hear and read. American scientists are encouraged to visit their colleagues overseas and to teach in foreign lands. Our laboratories and universities have been opened to foreign visitors coming by the thousands. Untold millions have been contributed to equip laboratories abroad. American science has done its part in rebuilding the international highways of science. This Russia has not done except in one week of self-gratifying celebration.

American science—in common with all phases of our culture—has accepted the responsibility to share its knowledge and its methods with all peoples, and especially with those who are victims of poverty and disease and ignorance. Western science has an important role in shaping world cultures appropriate for these times.

Modern cities with sanitation and communication and transportation are the products of science—but slums and noise and polluted air are symbols of our too great regard for the material aspects of civilization, and of too little regard for human life. Galley slaves, and those who toiled from dawn to dusk to build the pyramids, have been replaced by the American operators of machines, who create a vast flood of material goods; but the machine worker of mass production has not yet achieved a noble life of creation.

Certainly the solution is not to abandon science, for even those who deplore most loudly the evils of our machine age would reluctantly return to a life of ceaseless labor, hardship, and disease. The same machines that build the slums can recreate the cities for human welfare. The planes that carried bombs on their missions of destruction are also available for the swift transportation of sick and wounded.

If I were to name another and one of the most admirable characteristics of American culture, it would be the gradual union of the physical and the human sciences, and more especially the union of the natural sciences with the social sciences and the humanities. In these troubled days the scientists have little satisfaction in the social consequence of their discoveries. The material contributions of science alone do not create a rich and satisfying life. Nor do the intellectual values of science alone provide the spiritual satisfaction which men crave. Scientists are merely partners of many others in mankind's great endeavor. Science liberates men from the fear of unknown natural forces, frees men from grinding toil for mere survival, subdues pain and cures sickness. Thus, science frees men to enjoy art and music and literature and the beauties of nature and religious faith. Science makes possible the enjoyment of much that science alone cannot give. Scientists are partners of those in other walks of life who seek to improve man's estate.

I should be blind to the status of modern American science if I did not recognize its critics and opponents. Many are torn between *fear* of new horrors science may add and *hope* that science will build a better world. Without science which created the atomic bomb we should still be defenseless against natural forces and disease. Would we rather be the *certain* victims of natural forces or *possible* victims of atomic energy misused by man? The question is: Do we have courage to understand the facts of nature and educate our fellow men to use them for the welfare of mankind?

Science provides the building stones of a better world— but the world will be as we choose to make it.

CHAPTER IV

The Heritage of Idealism[*]

Brand Blanshard

TWENTIETH-CENTURY philosophy in America begins with idealism. At the turn of the century it was in the ascendant everywhere. Royce and Palmer at Harvard, Bowne at Boston, Ladd and Bakewell at Yale, Butler at Columbia, Ormond and Hibben at Princeton, Fullerton at Pennsylvania, Garman at Amherst, Everett at Brown, Creighton and Thilly at Cornell, Wenley and Lloyd at Michigan, Bascom at Wisconsin, Howison at California— they all spoke the same high language though with somewhat varying accents.

These idealists were a remarkable breed of men. They had never heard, to be sure, of protons or electrons; only too probably they had never heard of Freud or Pavlov or Frege. Since they had come into philosophy not from science, but from the humanities, their equipment on the scientific side was sometimes deplorable. Nor was their logic a very subtle instrument, by the standards of today.

---

[*] The course of the thought here follows roughly that of my chapter (76), "Speculative Thinkers," in *Literary History of the United States,* edited by R. E. Spiller, W. Thorp, T. H. Johnson, and H. S. Canby (New York: The Macmillan Company, 1948).

A passage at arms between one of these men and a present-day Cambridge analyst would be a little like the contest between Richard and Saladin in Scott's novel, in which there was a broadsword heavy as a cleaver on one side and on the other a scimitar so sharp that it would cut a down cushion in two.

But whatever their technical deficiencies, these idealists were wise men, wiser than many of their successors. Wisdom is of course a large word. What I mean is that they were more than learned men—though apart from science their learning was considerable—and more than clever reasoners—though they knew how to state a case. They were wise as Nestor and Goethe and Emerson were wise, weighty in counsel because they had thought much about the ends of living and looked upon the interests and aims of men from an altitude that gave perspective. Since they thought that mind was at the heart of things, they set themselves to explore what they took as their best clue, their own mind in its central areas, in religion, in reason, in moral choice, and in art. They were perceptive, humane, and versatile. I must confess to an initial prejudice in favor of the philosopher who, if he had not been a philosopher, would still have counted in the world in other ways, and these men would have counted for much. Wenley would have made a rare literary critic; Palmer was in fact both a classical scholar and a fine interpreter of literature; Royce was a man of magisterial learning; Hibben was a distinguished university head; Garman and Howison were unique as personalities. Philosophy for these idealists was not an avocation or a specialty but a way of life and the breath of life; it was a passionate pursuit of reasonableness in action and feeling as well as in thought. Indeed it was for them what it was for their contemporary Bradley, "a principal way of experiencing the Deity." McTaggart used to poke fun at such philosophers as persons who regarded a beefsteak merely as a means of gaining strength to appreciate Dante. And we must admit that when we read them today we find more of the prophet and the pontiff in them than suits our latter-day taste. They seem always to be writing in Prince Albert coats.

I have suggested that they stood for moral as well as philosophical idealism. But it is with their philosophy that we are concerned, and we must try at once to see what that philosophy was. For what we want to do is to learn what has happened in American thought in the last fifty years, and the fact is that all its main developments have come as reactions against the great system that held the field at the turn of the century. We must know what that system was if we are to catch the point or the reason of the passionate protests against it. Very well, what is idealism?

The idealism of the turn of the century was a fusion of two streams of thought. One of these, subjective idealism, took its rise in the ingenious mind of Bishop Berkeley and flowed down through Hume and Mill. The other, objective idealism, is as old as Plato and comes down through the Germany of Hegel, and the England of Green and

Bradley, to Josiah Royce in Harvard Yard. The first of these idealisms stands for the thesis, "All that is real is experience." The second stands for the thesis, "All that is real is rational." To see what American absolute idealism meant, we must see the meaning of both these theses.

There are few excitements in philosophy to compare with reading for the first time the argument for subjective idealism and feeling how powerful it is. Take any common thing, say an apple, and let it stand for nature as a whole. The argument of the idealist is an act of intellectual prestidigitation by which he undertakes to make the apple vanish as a physical thing and reappear as a bit of consciousness. The first step is to get you to admit that the apple, as you know it, is a set of sensed qualities. If you were to remove from the apple its redness and roundness, sweetness and hardness, coldness and smoothness, would there be any apple left? No. The perceived apple then is composed of these qualities? Yes. Where do these qualities reside? The idealist answers, "In consciousness," and he offers two main arguments.

First, the causal argument. Assume, as everyone does, that there is a physical apple out there. Clearly enough its existence is only a hypothesis; we never see or feel *it*. What we do see and feel is these sense data, but they apparently arise at the end of a long causal chain. Light rays strike our retinas and start nervous pulses there; these, when they reach our brains, give rise in some mysterious way to sensations of red and green. But these sensations come at the end of the chain, not at the beginning; responsible physicists would not hold that the red and green we see are out there in the source from which the light rays come; they are effects that arise in us. They have their independent causes, but to say this is already to admit the case, for then it becomes perfectly clear that you cannot identify the inner or conscious effect, the sensation of red for example, with the outward cause, which is separated from this effect by at least several feet in space and perhaps half a second in time. If this is true of the color, it is true equally of the other qualities. But if true of these, it is true of the apple as you know it, for you have admitted that it consists of these. And in that case what you have done is to shift this apple into consciousness. Indeed you have done a great deal more. You have done what Archimedes wanted to do; you have put a lever under experienced nature as a whole and heaved it across the boundary into mind. Rocks and rivers, clouds and mountains, the whole "choir of heaven and furniture of earth" as Berkeley called them, are seen to be "such stuff as dreams are made on." They arise and flourish and die within the realm of conscious experience.

The second argument for subjective idealism is as follows: Assume that qualities as we know them do really belong to physical things, and you end by contradicting yourself. The classic illustration is Locke's. You believe, do you, that the qualities given in sense really belong to the physical thing? Good; then, for example, the hots and colds you feel belong to the physical thing. But consider what follows. One of your hands has been resting on a hot-water bottle and the other on a block of ice; you plunge them both into a basin of water; the water feels cold to one hand and hot to the other. On your assumption, the water is both hot and cold, and that does not make sense. The idealist says that the most plausible way out is to admit that the hot and cold are not in the physical thing at all, but in our experience, for while it is incredible that the water is in any straightforward sense both hot and cold, there is no trouble at all in saying that at one time we can sense both hot and cold. And what is true of hots and colds is true of shapes and sizes. To say that all the shapes we see as we walk round a table, all the sizes that we see as our friend walks away from us down the street, belong out there in the thing is impossible in the ordinary sense of "belonging"; to hold that they are all appearances in our consciousness is a perfectly plausible belief. That is what the idealist did say. What did he take these arguments to show? Not, if he was self-critical, that there was nothing in nature but consciousness; they clearly do not prove that there is nothing "out there" at all to *cause* these appearances in our minds. Jeans and Eddington thought that the protons and electrons were mental also. Whether they were right or not it is immensely difficult to say. But as for the rocks and rivers, the hills and clouds, the frame of nature generally *as we directly know it,* the case of subjective idealism seems to me to have a higher plausibility than any alternative realism that has yet been offered.

Now what is *absolute* idealism? It is a philosophy, as we have said, whose principle is that the real is the rational.

How does it reach that belief? It does so through two steps, one of self-inspection and one of faith. Josiah Royce looked into his mind as he was philosophizing and asked himself what he was trying to do. The answer seemed clear enough; he was trying to understand the world. But what do you mean by understanding? You mean explaining to yourself. Yes, but when is a thing explained? It is explained, Royce answered, when you see not only *that* it is, but *why* it is, when you see that, given the conditions, it had to be what it is. When is the Pythagorean theorem explained? It is explained when you see that, given the postulates of Euclid, it follows with such necessity that if it were denied, the postulates and indeed the whole system would have to go with it. This, said Royce, is what you do when you try to understand anything; you place it in a system, and when you see that within that system it has to be what it is, you are satisfied. Now that, he said, is what philosophy tries to do for our whole world of common experience; it tries to find the system to which things belong and within which they are necessary and therefore intelligible. I have a philosopher-friend with a small daughter. She fell into discussion one day with a neighbor's boy about the relative merits of their fathers. "What does your father do?" said the boy, with a hoity-toity air. She had never thought about this, but after a moment's reflection she came up with, "His business is words." "What words?" said the boy scornfully. "He says Why?" was her reply. That is philosophy in three letters. Philosophy, as James said, is a peculiarly stubborn effort to think clearly; it is an insistent raising of the question why; and nothing short of a single intelligible system will set that question finally at rest. To see that is the first step in absolute idealism.

The second step is an act of faith. Suppose that by superhuman exertion and ability you did arrive at a system in which everything was apparently included and seen to be necessary; your intellectual ideal would be realized. But what surety have you that when you have reached what satisfies your own mind, you have also reached what is outwardly true? Is it not possible, as Kant believed, that we are all little metaphysical spiders, spinning webs which are much alike but bear no resemblance to the outward nature of things? Here is where faith comes in. The idealist does not, if he knows his business, try to juggle from his own hat a proof that the world is rational. What he says is more modest and more plausible. He says that philosophy is the attempt to understand the world—that is, to render it intelligible—that, unless the world really is so, the attempt must be defeated, and that it would be silly to accept defeat before it comes. The rationality of the world is not for him a proved conclusion but rather a postulate on which his enterprise proceeds and on whose truth its success depends.

This, then, is idealism. It holds that the world of colors, shapes, and sounds that each of us lives in is really the world of his own mind. But our minds are islands, "finite centers" as Bradley called them, in a larger world, and since the idealist believes this larger world to be rational through and through, he is inclined to think it too is mental or spiritual. For him the prime business of life is to escape his fragmentariness, to bring his own little spirit into closer approximation to the world spirit both in extent and in inward order. Like Marcus Aurelius, St. Paul, and Spinoza, his rationalism has usually run out into mysticism; and he has conceived the best hope for himself as lying in self-surrender to the reason that animates the nature of things. Only through becoming the servant of that reason could he become in the best sense free.

Such was the philosophy that had captured academic America in 1900. The fact of this capture was itself significant. Foreign critics had long been charging that the American soul had shriveled into an impulse after the dollar, adding that where there is no vision, the people perish. It should perhaps have seemed odder than it did that a product of these money-grabbers and indeed their favorite prophet should have been the idealist Emerson, and that when they turned to philosophy professionally, they became idealists with such uniformity. The fact is that along with our preoccupation with practice, which ill-disposed critics persist in miscalling materialism, there has always gone in the American mind a strain of moral idealism and religious seriousness to which such thought is congenial. Probably idealism triumphed in the schools largely because it set this religious chord of our nature in strong vibration. Americans, like Englishmen of a generation before, were worried about what Darwinism would do to their faith, and here was a philosophy which told them with authority that Darwin was not the last word, that scientifically he might be right, but philosophically and therefore fundamentally there was nothing in what he said to shake the walls of their spiritual city. There are neo-Freudians who like to think that when they have discovered this consolatory element in idealism they have refuted the philosophy by explaining it away. They have chosen their ground strategically. They would get short shrift from a thinker of Royce's stature if they tried to meet him on his own ground. To attack someone else's philosophy by imputing motives never refutes it, though it not seldom raises suspicions about one's own.

Still, it is true that the appeal of idealism was largely to religious wistfulness, that in the last fifty years this wistfulness has been fast fading from the American mind, and that to the hardier temper of the later decades idealism is uncongenial. To the natural man the belief that the world is spirit has always seemed incredible, and in a country like our own, where action presses hard upon contemplation, the strange thing is that so uncompromising a system of speculative thought should have achieved the hold it did.

The inevitable revolt soon came. When it did, it was not a local rebellion so much as a general rising in which guerrillas sprang up behind every bush. Soon idealism was engaged in confused battle everywhere, and as the guerrillas coalesced, there appeared the schools that hold the field in America today. To some critics the head and front of idealist offending was the notion that the world was spirit; their rebellion became the new naturalism. Some found their special aversion in the idea of an Absolute and of a fixed framework for the world; these were the pragmatists, whose revolt is now being absorbed into logical positivism. With others the point of attack was subjectivism, and here the revolt developed into two new schools of realism. All these attacks were carried on simultaneously, but in order to make a complicated tale as straight as may be, we shall take the three main revolts in order. First, naturalism.

In Royce's classes at Harvard was a dark and reserved young man with a Spanish accent, who listened to the master with respect but with skeptical detachment. His name was George Santayana. Born in Spain of Spanish parents and coming to this country at nine without knowing a word of English, he seems to have felt himself from the first an alien, and with an ultra-Castilian pride to have delighted in remaining a pilgrim and stranger. For forty years he lived in this country, observing American ways with his shrewd, appraising eyes, reading voraciously in the Harvard library, lecturing reluctantly to youth, who hardly knew what to make of him, absorbing the language with such discrimination as to become one of the great masters of English prose. "It is as an American writer that I must be counted," he says. But he did not like America. He disliked its democracy, its puritanism, its Protestantism, its restless activity, its extroversion, its loudness, its apparently permanent adolescence. When in 1912 a small legacy enabled him to give up his professorship, he took ship for Europe and never set foot on American shores again.

It is natural that, disliking puritanism as he did, he should distrust the philosophies in which it found expression. Idealism he could not abide. It made mind or spirit the center of things, and if there is one conviction that runs from first to last in Santayana's writings, it is that spirit is only the by-product of matter. The idealist makes matter an appearance within mind. The plain man thinks that matter and mind are both real and act on each other—that mind acts on body whenever he wills, and body on mind whenever he steps on a tack. For Santayana neither suggestion will do. He not only denies that mind is all; he denies that it has any substantial existence or the slightest influence on matter; matter is the only substance there is. He does not, to be sure, deny that consciousness exists, but he holds that it is a sort of phosphorescence on the surface of the brain that glows and fades with the changing arrangements of the protons and electrons; it is, as he puts it, "a lyric cry in the midst of business," "a wanton music" babbled by the flow of energy in the brain. Most of us think that when we will to lift a hand or to give an opinion, our purpose has some influence in making our body do what it does. Santayana says no; the purpose makes no difference; it is merely the conscious glow attending the real cause, which is the physical process in the brain. Most of us think that at times we make a free

choice. Santayana says no; we never do. Most of us think
that when we follow a chain of reasoning, the fact that
the premises are in our mind has something to do with
the appearance of what follows. Santayana says no; it
never does; the sequence of our thoughts is governed
wholly by the movements of matter in our heads.

In his youth evolution was the great new idea, and he
found in it timely support for his materialism. The roots
that man has in nature are very long roots that run down
through the animal mind; indeed we are all animals
whose science and poetry, religion and art, disguise it as
we may, are the flowering of animal impulse. Whatever
flower of the spirit does not spring from such impulse
springs from an insane root. The Greeks saw that. The
early Christians, the Stoics, the Transcendentalists, the
Puritans did not; they lost sight of the true end of man,
which is not to save a nonexistent soul, but to make the
most of the little capital of years and energy that a nig-
gardly nature has allowed. These people were fanatics,
a fanatic being a man who redoubles his effort when he
has forgotten his aim. Sanity lies in recognizing that
"everything ideal has a natural basis and everything natural an ideal development." This is the text, taken from
Aristotle, which Santayana embroidered and celebrated
through the five volumes of *The Life of Reason,* and
which he insists, as against some critics, is the main theme
of his four later volumes on *The Realm of Essence.* What
we have in these massive works is an enchantingly intoned
philosophy of disenchantment, in which the great specula-

tive systems of the past are waved aside with an incredulous smile, and all the religious beliefs of mankind are dealt with in the spirit of that gently withering remark of John Morley's: "We do not refute Christianity, we explain it."

The materialism of Santayana, however disillusioned, is the philosophy of a sensitive, mellow, and deeply brooding mind. But a year after he set sail for Europe there appeared in the *Philosophical Review* the first manifesto of another kind of materialism. It was entitled "Psychology from the Standpoint of a Behaviorist" and bore the name of John B. Watson. Not long afterward came a book with the same title in which the preface contained this statement—surely an odd one for a work on psychology: "the reader will find no discussion of consciousness and no reference to such terms as sensation, perception, will, image, and the like. . . . I have found that I can get along without them." Why so curious a self-denying ordinance? It was not mere perversity. Watson was a scientist, and he wanted his science of mind to be truly scientific. If it is to be truly scientific, he said, it must be able to lay down laws that are precise and publicly verifiable. Was the psychology of the time able to do that? No, he answered; you could search the fat volumes of James and Wundt, Ward and Titchener, without finding a single law of the kind required. And why the failure? It was because they used the wrong method, the method of introspection. No observation you can make about your own will or emotions can ever be exact, in the sense of measurable, nor can it be objective in the sense that it can be checked by anyone else. If psychology is to become a science, then, it must turn its back on introspection. Where is it to turn instead? Watson believed that he had found the answer in his own graduate study at Chicago on the behavior of rats. Here he had found that generalizations of high accuracy and predictive power could be derived from observing bodily reactions to carefully determined stimuli. Thorndike had been moving toward similar conclusions as a result of a study, made in William James's cellar at Cambridge, of how cats and dogs escaped from cages; and there was further encouragement in rumors that came from Pavlov's laboratory in St. Petersburg. Why should not the methods that had been so successful with animals be applied with like success to man?

Watson did not at first claim that his behaviorism was anything more than a method, but it soon became clear that if a method appropriate only to bodily behavior was really adequate to the study of mind, then mind *was* only bodily behavior. Watson bravely drew the inference. "If behaviorism is ever to stand for anything (even a distinct method)," he wrote, "it must make a clean break with the whole concept of consciousness." This "has never been seen, touched, smelled, tasted, or moved. It is a plain assumption, just as unprovable as the old concept of the soul." Here the pendulum had swung from idealism all the way to the opposite extreme; the consciousness that had started by being all-embracing, was now denied any place at all. For a time the new doctrine had great vogue, seeping into graduate schools throughout the country and leading Count Keyserling to the gibe that it was the fitting psychology for a people without inner life. But since about 1930 the tide has been receding. It is not merely that the achievements of the new method turned out to be less illuminating than those of the older introspection in the hands of men who could use it, like William and Henry James; it is also that we have come to see that behaviorism, as Professor Broad has observed, is a "silly philosophy." It is in truth merely "old-fashioned materialism that has crossed the Atlantic under an alias"; he would no doubt take it as an example of his rule that all good fallacies go to America when they die. To hold, as Santayana does, that a toothache or a moral choice is conditioned by the movements of matter in the brain at least makes sense; but to say that the toothache or the choice *is* those physical movements and nothing besides is to say what any clear-headed person can see to be absurd. Unfortunately the absurd, as a philosopher of note has remarked, may have this in common with truth, that it cannot be refuted. If anyone maintains that he means by a toothache nothing but the motions of matter in his head and sticks to this, he is beyond the reach of mere logic. Still, nonsense that is irrefutable is none the less truly nonsense.

The naturalism of the present day has for the most part discarded behaviorism and taken its cue from Santayana rather than from Watson. To be sure, Santayana was not accepted as a prophet in his own New England; his philosophy was not congenial either to the earlier Puritan Boston or to the Catholic Boston of today. It has taken a firmer root in New York, where it has deeply influenced the thought of a group of Columbia philosophers, particularly Woodbridge, Montague, Edman, and Randall. The latest manifesto of the naturalists appeared in 1944, under the title *Naturalism and the Human Spirit,* a book by fifteen American philosophers, most of whom had been at Columbia as students or teachers. This Columbian naturalism agrees with behaviorism in holding that there are not two different kinds of stuff, matter and mind; there is really only one, matter. On the other hand, matter has a far larger and more sophisticated repertory of parts than old-fashioned mechanists supposed. Hydrogen and oxygen singly behave like gases; put them together and they make a liquid; their behavior is the function of their new partnership. Go on increasing the complexity of such unions and, without any change of nature, you get behavior that is intelligent and purposive. And then lo! we have mind. Mind is not another kind of stuff than matter. It is the same stuff precisely, but acting in more complicated ways. Whatever nature's robe, it is a seamless one.

What are we to say of these American naturalists? Every fair-minded reader must, I think, read them with sympathy. They never speak from Mount Sinai, as some of the idealists did; they are remarkably free from the self-delusions of wishful thinking; they are trying to be austerely honest with themselves and the evidence. Life has taken for them a sober coloring from eyes that have kept watch over the stark facts of man's mortality. They are modest, candid, and humane. Nevertheless, their philosophy has not gained general acceptance, and I doubt if it ever will. For the truth is that the new naturalism is false to fact and in the end false to itself.

It is false to fact in that it tries to bridge the deepest chasm in nature with words. It says that the life of mind—thinking, choosing, feeling—is a more complicated bodily behaving, differing from that of H_2O in the same sort of way as that differs from the behavior of H *or* O. And this is untrue. In the very simplest sensation or feeling you have something utterly different from the motions of particles, and since it is different in kind, you cannot reach it—you cannot even come nearer to it—by complicating the pattern of these motions. When they criticize behaviorism, the new naturalists seem to see this clearly. When they turn to criticize the dualists, who hold to a radical difference between consciousness and behavior, they take it all back and insist that if you regard consciousness as a function of body and not as different in kind, a great light dawns and you see how two can be one. Their vision is a little like that of St. Theresa who once, in a mystic opening, saw how the three persons of the Trinity could be one. Unfortunately, when she saw it she had arrived at such an altitude that she could not explain it when she came down. The lips of our newer naturalists seem to have been sealed in the same sad way.

But falsity to fact is not the worst flaw of naturalism, for it is also false to reason. It makes all rational thought, including its own, a miracle. When we set ourselves to pursue a course of reasoning, for example in geometry, we try to follow a line of logical implication from proposition to proposition, and we succeed just so far as we can surrender ourselves to it, let it tell its own story, allow our thought to be placed under constraint by the logic of the case. We can see that to allow the course of our thought or our acceptance of a conclusion to be determined by nonrational pulls would be fatal to the whole enterprise of reason; it would make the reaching of any valid conclusion a matter of luck. Now this is exactly what naturalism does. "The controlling force in reasoning," writes Santayana, "is not reason, but instinct and circumstance"; "the continuity is physical, not logical." But here surely disillusionment has come full circle and shown that it is itself an illusion. If, when Santayana argues for the truth of naturalism, it is not reason but something nonrational, what he calls "the dark engine of the body," that governs his thought and determines his conclusion, why should we accept that conclusion? To urge the conclusion upon us as one that is irrationally arrived at, and to accompany this with the comment that no argument for it will be able to move us in the least, is a strange way to recommend any theory. Yet it is all that is left to Santayana. *The Life of Reason* is a resplendent drama in five acts in which the hero, reason, is retired to the wings at the beginning and we realize, little by little, that it is all a marvelous puppet show in which none of the characters has ever been moved by a feeling or an idea. Santayana sincerely accepts this as an account of how his own magnificent work has been achieved, just as Poe seems to have believed that poetic impulse had nothing to do with the creation of "The Raven." But in accepting it he has exchanged a supernaturalist mythology which at least satisfied the imagination for a naturalist mythology which satisfies neither imagination nor thought. If this is naturalism, we may leave it to take care of itself.

But naturalism has not been the only, or indeed the most interesting, revolt against idealism. To another and contemporary rebellion belongs the credit of having produced the only important original philosophy that has appeared on American soil. This is pragmatism. What turned the pragmatists against idealism was partly its absolutism, the notion that the world was a "block-universe"—a finished, timeless system, a marble temple shining on a hill—and partly its intellectualism, its view that thinking was an activity with ends of its own, which could be carried on in complete independence of action. In a sense the two objections are the same. The idealist said that to philosophize was to try to construe experience into a system all-inclusive and intelligible, and if you ever reached that system, it would be the absolute. The pragmatist replied that the absolutism of the idealist arose from his intellectualism, that he first built up an ideal of what would satisfy his intellect, and then projected this ideal upon the face of the world. Only one thing is necessary, then, to bring down the idealist's house about his ears, namely, to show that he has made a mistake about the goal of thought. The attempt to show this has been the main endeavor of John Dewey. Dewey had the hardihood to deny that thought was aiming at intelligible system at all. The truth is, he said, that thought is merely another *instrument* like walking or talking whose value is its utility in adjusting men to nature and to each other. This is why he called his theory instrumentalism.

At the name of John Dewey we must pause for a salute. He is the most considerable figure in the history of academic American philosophy. There could hardly be a greater contrast than that between the leader of the naturalistic and the leader of the pragmatic revolt. Santayana was an alien, a patrician, a poet, a hermit, a detached and amused contemplator of men and their queer ways. Dewey had his roots deep in American ground; he is a plebeian in his thinking, writing, and sympathies; he believes that philosophy should issue in practice, and his own has issued in the courageous defense of all sorts of causes from socialism at home to the forlorn cause of Trotsky in Mexico. What makes his immense influence the more remarkable is that it has been won without any of the outward address that commonly belongs to the man of large following. His style fumbles and shuffles; there is little play of humor, no sparkle, no command of the arts or graces. He is the Vermont farmer, intellectually outsize, speaking in homely fashion from a deeply thoughtful and honest mind. Part of his vast influence is due to the sheer length of time through which he has sustained his indefatigable fertility; he came into the world while Washington Irving was still writing at Sunnyside and James Buchanan was in the White House. But more important than the volume of Dewey's work is that the man was matched with the time. The retreat of idealism was leaving an "ideological" vacuum; pragmatism poured into it with a philosophy of practice that suited the American mood, impatient as it is of contemplation and logical finesse, and exigent of results.

William James called pragmatism "a new name for old ways of thinking." Something a little like it had been suggested as long ago as Protagoras, and among Americans it had been proposed in different forms by C. S. Peirce and by James himself. But Peirce was a logician who winced and shrank as he listened to James's exposition of their supposedly common creed. And no wonder. William James, superb psychologist and great man that he was, was not a metaphysician and gave some very strange exhibitions when he tried to be. In 1896 he wrote a famous essay, "The Will to Believe," in which he laid down a doctrine welcomed by beleaguered theologians as a new and powerful defensive weapon. If you have to make up your mind on a religious issue, say that of immortality, and find that you do not know enough to settle it yourself and that even the doctors disagree, then you are entitled, said James, to adopt as true whatever belief has the most desirable consequences. This seemed innocent enough, since it included the proviso that we were to fall back on such consequences only when the logical evidence failed us. Nevertheless, Bertrand Russell has branded the doctrine as immoral, as encouraging us to believe on evidence which we know to be irrelevant, and with this I can only agree. But James, instead of seeing that he had gone too far and beating a retreat, went stubbornly on, and was soon maintaining that belief generally was justified by the consequences of accepting it. If the belief in an Absolute worked for you, then even that was true. The truth of a belief not only was tested by, but consisted in, its consequences; the belief literally became true or false as these consequences unrolled.

The philosophic world discussed this well-meant doctrine with an ill-concealed twinkle in its eye. "So you really think, do you, that if an old lady has lived happily all her years in the conviction that immortality is true, that tends to make it true? Did the belief that the earth is round become true for the first time when a believer circumnavigated the globe? If you believe that the 8:10 train is an 8:30 train, and, arriving twenty minutes late, find the train delayed and catch it anyhow, does the happy ending prove that you were right all along?" These were obvious difficulties, and James had a miserable time in meeting them; the fact was that he did not and could not meet them; he had never thought his pragmatism through. If he had, he would have seen that it is only under highly special circumstances that the results of a belief have anything to do with its truth.

Now the great advance made by Dewey is to see this and provide for it. He provides for it by reinterpreting the aim of thinking. If he could show that the aim of thought was precisely to secure certain consequences and not, as had always been supposed, to lay bare the nature and structure of things, if thinking could be construed as a device for enabling us to control things to our advantage, then success in gaining this advantage would give the very meaning of truth. If it could be shown that the belief in God, so far as it had a meaning at all, was a "plan of action" devised to carry us through to certain ends in the way of personal and social harmony, then these results were, after all, relevant in a way they never were in the groping philosophy of James.

Dewey set himself to this reinterpretation of the nature of thought. His starting point was the theory of evolution. Born in the year of the *Origin of Species,* and author of a book on *The Influence of Darwin on Philosophy,* he has himself been described as the influence of Darwin on philosophy. He pointed out that, in the history of the race, thought must have come into being as a tool of survival. For primitive man, as someone has even argued of ourselves, life is a conjugation of the verb "to eat" in the active and the passive; and when he had to catch some game or starve, necessity proved the mother of invention and gave birth to a bow and arrow. Thought here is plainly a means to ends which are to be realized through action. If we only took the blinkers from our eyes, we should see that it is so still, and that the use of it by traditional philosophy is a means of theoretical indulgence, and—Dewey commonly adds in an acidulated footnote—

self-indulgence on the part of a quite dispensable leisure class.

This bold reconceiving of the nature and end of thought seems to me the most original note in American philosophy. Has Dewey made out his case? Most philosophers think not. Instrumentalism has taken root nowhere outside America, unless Karl Marx, whose view of the true function of thought is surprisingly like Dewey's, is read as a pragmatist. We have seen that James was an acute psychologist who had to rely on Dewey to rescue him when he turned to metaphysics. One can only add, unhappily, that the rope his good friend threw him turned out to be made of psychological tow. Dewey's view of thought as an instrument of behavior or plan of action seems to most sober critics pretty wild. To say that a judgment about the length of Cleopatra's nose, or the thousandth decimal of *pi,* or a clash of colors in Picasso, or the Trinity, is an instrument directed to some future end and a means of initiating action toward that end has so low a plausibility as to have left most students cool, even in a country where action and results are certainly not undervalued. Outside America few philosophers of standing have taken the trouble to refute it.

Pragmatism is dying. But its soul is undergoing a fissiparous transmigration into a numerous and diverse progeny. The parental features keep cropping out in law, history, education, and scientific method.

In law they appear at the top in the features of one of the best-known justices of the Supreme Court, who was a lifelong friend of James, Oliver Wendell Holmes. In the days of the New Deal, there was tension within that august court itself between those who sought to protect property rights against government incursions, and those who held that if these "rights" were at odds with the general advantage, they should go. Holmes was the leader of this last group and an avowed pragmatist in the law. "The true grounds of decision," he wrote, "are considerations of policy and of social advantage, and it is vain to suppose that solutions can be attained merely by logic. . . ." "There is nothing I deprecate more than the use of the fourteenth amendment . . . to prevent the making of social experiments. . . ." To call this position pragmatism, however, is likely to mislead; it is more properly described as legal utilitarianism. Pragmatism holds that *truth* depends on consequences; utilitarianism holds that *right* depends on consequences; that the views have an affinity is suggested by James's dedication of his *Pragmatism* to John Stuart Mill. All pragmatists are utilitarians of one stripe or another. But of course one can accept the consequences view in ethics without accepting it also in logic; that has in fact been the position of nine utilitarians out of ten, including Mill himself.

Pragmatism has had its influence on historical as well as legal thinking. One of the pioneers of what is called "The New History" was a friend and follower of Dewey's, James Harvey Robinson, whose Columbia course on the history of the intellectual class in Europe was widely taken as a model. Robinson, like Dewey, developed a profound distrust of all speculative thinking, and in his little book on *The Mind in the Making* of 1921 developed the same theory that Dewey did a year earlier in his *Reconstruction of Philosophy,* namely, that the religious and metaphysical theories of the past are the product of causes rather than reasons, that as a rule they are "rationalizations" which are hardly to be taken with intellectual seriousness, and that they can be explained by the nonrational pushes and pulls of the time. This view seemed to accord with the results of the new sociology and anthropology. Such prolific workers in these fields as Boas and Malinowski, Lowie, Goldenweiser, and Margaret Mead, were impressing upon the public mind that there was hardly a belief, however irrational, or a practice, however absurd, that had not somewhere been solemnly approved. The natural inference was that both speculative and moral beliefs were relative to time and place. It became part of the standard mental apparatus of university students to be thus "sophisticated"; the claim for any moral law that it was universally or objectively right seemed provincial; there was a large tolerance about the new relativism that spoke to the generous instincts of youth. But when tolerance goes over into indifference it is not a virtue, and this view did notable disservice to youth in the days between the wars. When international gangsterism raises its head, conviction is an even greater need than tolerance. In such cases a little philosophy is a dangerous thing, and I am convinced that the trouble with ethical relativism is, as a rule, its naïveté. It forgets that differing customs may be differing means to the same end; that the ends men prize —their scale of values—are pretty much the same everywhere; and that there is no good reason to believe that the basic judgments of that scale—that happiness is better than misery, for example, or knowledge than ignorance— are less than universally and objectively true.

I think, then, that the pragmatic account of philosophy, and its confederate, the sociological account of ethics, may be ruled out by what has been called "the law of excluded muddle." But what are we to say of that other influence of pragmatism which goes so much further than either of those we have mentioned, its influence on education? Dewey's is today the great name in the philosophy of education. Now education is chiefly the training of intelligence, and since Dewey has swung his immense influence to a new view of what intelligence is for, his impact on American education has been formidable. Conceive intelligence as an instrument of practical adjustment and you must reconceive education to suit. Culture in Arnold's sense will cease to be an end. Such cultural subjects of the older curriculum as pure mathematics must obviously be demoted. Philosophy as the pursuit of truth for its own sake will be abandoned; such philosophy, as opposed to the newer pragmatic discipline, bakes no bread.

What is to be included instead? It is hard to secure a definite answer. Professor Kilpatrick says: What one needs to know in order to do what one needs to do. Since, in the pragmatist view, "to learn is to acquire a way of behaving," education should equip us with the most useful ways of behaving. And since men's walks in life have more directions than the spokes of a wheel, the curriculum will become hospitable to an immense variety of technical and vocational subjects, and the line between these and the cultural subjects will be obliterated; in some liberal arts colleges where the influence of this theory is strongest, one can apparently "major" in photography or the dance. Again the theory calls for change not only in subject-matter but in method. Since thinking is essentially doing, the way to learn anything is to do it. It is through the application of this view in "progressive education" that pragmatism has had its widest schoolroom influence. In a thousand progressive schools, children began to learn their arithmetic by playing store, biology by raising plants and keeping pets, literature by "creative writing" and the staging of plays. The way to sustain such activity is to make it interesting, and the way to make it interesting is to make it an obvious means to an end to which the child is devoted; he will then provide his own discipline. The ideal, one expositor says, is neither "the hard pedagogy of doing what you don't like, nor the soft pedagogy of doing what you like, but the new pedagogy of liking what you do."

Is it to be wondered at that this pragmatic theory of education swept through American schools like a prairie fire? The little red schoolhouse, however romanticized, was about as far behind modern needs as the old oaken bucket; to countless eager youngsters it proved a strait jacket which gave them a fixed repugnance to the whole business of education; its subjects and its methods cried out for revision. This Dewey and his followers have given it, to the great relief of the pupils and, I suspect, to their advantage. Indeed just as the pragmatic theory of intelligence does approximately hold for the youth of the race, so the pragmatic theory of education holds for the youth of the individual. Healthy children are sturdy pragmatists, and it is no doubt well to treat them accordingly. But the pragmatic program, effective enough in the lower schools, has proved unconvincing when applied to higher education. Its implication that there is something a little abnormal about the interest of the mature scholar who would understand nature, human nature, and society just for the light it gives him, its suggestion that there is something snobbish about the desire for a rich and sensitive mind for its own priceless sake and apart from any dubious appeals to utility, seem to some of us like a defense of arrested development. However that may be, higher education is turning against the pragmatic theory. It is abandoning the elective system; it is insisting that liberal education should have some common content in standards and principles; and in the infinite, enticing complexity of the modern world, it is refusing to accept the view that the scholar's or scientist's intelligence is merely a tool for improving his lot. It is that, to be sure, but it is also very much more.

To infer from all this that pragmatism is dead would be a mistake. Just as it was beginning to show signs of debility, it received a blood transfusion from an unlikely donor across the sea. In the years between the wars a little coterie of mathematicians and physicists—Wittgenstein, Schlick, Carnap, Neurath, Frank—used to gather in Vienna and discuss over their steins the new world that was dawning in physics and the sense in which we could know it. Of course, no one has ever seen electrons or waves of radiation, and presumably no one ever will. What then are we talking about when we discuss them? These men found themselves moving toward a common view that they described as logical positivism or empiricism.

That view is roughly this: All knowledge is of two kinds. On the one hand is a priori knowledge, such knowledge as we have in those two great disciplines which philosophers have so often taken as their models, logic and mathematics, now seen to be one continuous science. It used to be supposed that they gave us our clearest and most certain knowledge of the framework of the world, but unfortunately they give us no knowledge of the world at all. An a priori statement merely says that we propose to use one symbol with the same meaning, in whole or part, as some other symbol. In "2 + 2 = 4," "4" is just another way of saying what we mean by "2 + 2." So of all logic and mathematics, and so of all philosophy so far as it consists of a priori knowledge. On the other hand there is empirical knowledge, knowledge of matters of fact. What does this refer to? Here the positivists came forward with their most original suggestion. They said that whenever we speak of a matter of fact, what we mean is the sensory observations that would verify it as true.

When the physicist says that atoms are constituted thus and so, what he really means is not some unimaginable x; he means that under specified conditions he will observe certain pointer-readings; these are what verify his statement. When the man lost in the woods concludes that the path before him leads to an exit, he means that if he follows the path he will see the exit. At first glance, like James's theory, this seems innocent enough. In fact, it means the wholesale abandonment of speculative philosophy as meaningless and a return to something like pragmatism under a new type of leadership, that of scientists and mathematical logicians. In their hostility toward metaphysics the two movements have joined hands. Dewey rejects absolutes and first causes and rational necessities and God because thought about these things does not run out into differences in practice. The logical positivists reject them because thought about them refers to nothing in sense. As philosophies, or antiphilosophies, the two movements come out in the same place, the renunciation of philosophy as traditionally conceived. For the pragmatists this sudden succor was an uncovenanted blessing sweeping in from an alien world.

Even in their ethics the pragmatists got support from the positivists, indeed rather more than they cared for. To the pragmatist, the statement that A is better than B is an expression not of rational insight but of psychological preference, and hence he could read without a qualm the views of sociologists like Sumner and Westermarck, who held it meaningless to call anything objectively better or worse than anything else. The positivists put this relativism in new and precise terms. Suppose you say "That act is right"; what, they asked, are you saying? Your statement is not a priori, for it is not a statement of what you mean by "that act," nor is it empirical, for rightness cannot be sensed. Therefore, say the positivists, it is not a statement at all; it is merely an expression of feeling like "Great guns!" or "Oh boy!"; their theory is known in some quarters as "the hurrah theory" of ethics. It follows that there is no such thing as objective right or wrong, and no kind of conduct that, strictly speaking, is more reasonable than any other. This view has had some odd results. Most of its exponents were anti-Nazis who before long became refugees. They disapproved of Hitler emphatically, and courageously said so. When their students pointed out to them that on their theory they had no rational or objective basis for this whatever, and that cruelty would become right, in the only sense in which anything is right, if Hitler's views gained general assent, some of them were much embarrassed. And well they might be. They have no adequate answer here. Their moral philosophy leaves their moral convictions in the air, with no visible means of support. Confronted with such ethical solipsism on the part of their new allies, the pragmatists, social crusaders all, have hardly known whether to acclaim them or to look the other way.

It will be evident from the space I have given it that pragmatism seems to me the central movement of American thought in the past half century. Its influence has been enormous, and in some fields, particularly those of politics and of elementary education, that influence seems to me to have been salutary. On the whole, however, I should incline to place pragmatism among the misadventures of ideas. Its central teaching about the nature of thought is too freakish to convince. At a time when Americans needed a firm directing scale of values, its vagueness about ends and its uninhibited experimentalism encouraged the idea that one study or activity was about as good as the next. It depreciated culture, of which we all need more, in favor of activity, of which most of us need less. It has tended to water down logic into the psychology of thinking, ethics into the study of behavior, religion into the psychology of an illusion or at best "the enthusiasm of humanity." Its attempt to discredit what for twenty centuries philosophers have approved as the business of reason has increased the difficulty of any common understanding among American philosophers, and between them and the outside world, while its prevailing laxity in both logic and language has depressed the level of our reflective writing.

To round out the story, I must give some brief account of the third revolt against idealism, that of the realists. You will remember what a plausible case the idealists made out that the apple as we know it, and for that matter rocks, rivers, and mountains too, were all really bits of consciousness. Sooner or later that violent paradox was bound to be repudiated. In America the repudiation was made with gusto in 1912 when a group of six influential philosophers published a joint manifesto entitled *The New Realism*. They insisted that the idealist argument was merely a piece of legerdemain, and that if you looked attentively you could see what was happening plainly enough. The idealist argued that the red of the apple was a sensation, and that since sensations were clearly mental, so was the color. But he failed to note that a sensation has two sides. On the one hand it is an act of awareness. Now this act—my sensing of red—*is* mental, as the idealist says. But then on the other hand there is the object sensed, in this case the red. And regarding this object there is not even a presumption that it is mental. What the idealist has done is to lump the act and the object together as we do in common speech, and say that because one component is mental, the whole is mental. He is offering us scandalous confusion as metaphysical profundity.

If you can thus distinguish the mental act from the nonmental red, you can do it, the realists added, with everything else. So they proceeded to unpack the entire contents of consciousness and push them out into nature again. Shapes and sizes they evicted with confidence. Colors, odors, and tastes took a little more courage, but they had it, and gave to these also a united and delighted heave-ho. The most extreme of them went further still, and insisted that nature was dotted in appropriate spots with toothaches, bent spoons, and pink rats. Then the movement began to disintegrate. The more cautious members complained that the trouble with realism, as with totalitarianism, was that it never knew when to stop. Start with the distinction, which seems so forthright, between the act of sensing and what you sense, place all the "whats" in the physical world, and where do you end? You end in something dangerously like absurdity, for what you are then saying is not only that the color you see is out there; you are saying that all the queer shapes you see when you walk round a chair and all the sizes you see when you walk away from it, all the rats and bats that alcoholics see on lost week ends, all the Jills and Jacks and beanstalks of our imagination, have a permanent being of their own apart from our awareness of them. Most philosophers think this wild, and I agree; but it does offer an alternative to idealism that is not logically impossible, and American realists might well have worked it out. In fact they were afraid of it. Only one of them would go all the way, Edwin Holt, who, having announced the discovery of round squares out in nature, gave it all up and turned to psychology. As for the rest of the gallant six, Perry, Montague, and Spaulding each developed a more qualified view of his own; Marvin withdrew from the life of reason to become a dean; and Walter Pitkin, an epistemologist of promise, found that new life could begin at forty.

What destroyed American new realism was its inability to deal with error and illusion. Meanwhile British realism, in the irrepressible person of Bertrand Russell, has shown what might have been done. He has had the courage to define a physical thing as the class of its appearances, and to say that it consists of all the sense-data that anyone could sense if he regarded "it" from any angle or at any distance; all these appearances exist, whether anyone perceives them or not. He would agree with Holt that the rats and bats of the alcoholic do not depend on being perceived, and to the objection that not all of us can see them he would reply that they exist only from certain points and instants, and unless we can occupy a point-instant of vantage, we shall surely miss them. This view, like every other theory of perception, has enormous difficulties. But Russell is a very clear head who knows that subjectivism is not avoidable unless you go to great lengths, who admits that realism is a bold hypothesis, and who holds that in this perilous problem of perception it is logic, not common sense, that must have the final vote.

In 1920 American realism returned to the attack under new leadership and from a fresh quarter; it presented a second joint manifesto with the title *Essays in Critical Realism*. Among the seven names on the title page were those of Santayana, who was now turning his attention to the theory of knowledge, and of Arthur Oncken Lovejoy, who is considered by some to be the acutest critical mind that America has produced. These seven were convinced that between idealism, which imported the object into consciousness, and the realism of their predecessors, which left it in outer nature while holding that we perceived it directly, there was a middle course more plausible than either extreme. There *is* a physical object; of that they were as certain as their predecessors. But what we perceive is not literally part of it; it is absurd to say that the shapes we see as we walk around a table are all out there in the thing; indeed the stuff of our percepts is identical with the stuff of our dreams; perception, says Santayana, is a sort of dreaming awake. But if this is true, how do we know that our percepts ever correspond to what exists out there? We never do, Santayana answers. We cannot even prove that there *is* a table out there; it is conceivable that the whole of external nature is an illusion. But possible though this is, it would be silly to take it seriously. The experience of millenniums has forced on us an "animal faith," and if we go on the assumption it offers us, we find that later experience confirms it. That assumption is that there exists out there apart from us an order in space and time, with tables and trees and mountains of fixed shape and regular behavior. Some of our percepts correspond to these things; some do not; we come by trial and error to learn which can be relied on. Our animal faith could not have carried us through unless it were largely true. Truth is the correspondence of our percepts or ideas with the nature of things; error is unwitting divergence.

This was a far more defensible realism than the one that preceded it, and in the finest book of the school, Lovejoy's *The Revolt Against Dualism,* it was defended with great subtlety and force. Unfortunately, as before, there were signs of a coming rift even in its first manifesto. Granting that the content of sense is not part of the physical thing, what is it exactly, and where in nature does it belong? On this issue the critical realists broke into opposing schools.

One, led by R. W. Sellars of the University of Michigan, held that our percepts are mental by-products of our brains, which came into being and passed away as the brain-state varied. The other wing, led by Santayana, developed a modern Platonism which aroused among his naturalist followers some astonishment and dismay. It held that the shapes and sizes, the colors and sounds we perceive are eternal essences, not dependent on being experienced and neither mental nor physical; when they swim into our ken, they are commonly taken as belonging to objects outside us; and they sometimes do, for they embody themselves in things as well as in experience. But they belong in a realm of their own; they never began; they will never cease to be; they are as timeless as the multiplication table. It is not for naturalists only that this theory has perplexities. Perhaps the gravest of these arises from Santayana's insistence that the essences are "vestal virgins," which neither suffer violence by mankind nor bear issue in practice. To most philosophers it seems clear that they do have issue in practice; that, as embodied in our ideas, they make an immense difference to the course of our thought, and, as embodied in things, to the course of nature. However that may be, critical realism, like its predecessor, has now succumbed to internal fission and hardly exists any longer as a distinct school. The theory of knowledge it offered is, nevertheless, the most sophisticated that America has produced, and its exponents have sharpened the edge of our philosophic self-criticism.

The story of our recent philosophy, as I have told it, consists of a series of revolts against speculative idealism. American thinkers, as the years have gone on, have become more strongly convinced that in view of the new techniques in logic and the esoteric developments of physics, they must watch their step. The day of the grand style in philosophy seemed to be over; cosmic systems and world spirits must give way to the minute philosophers. Our thought for half a century has been engaged in battering at the walls of the older speculative philosophy, and as the triumphant bands of attackers have marched round their Jericho, watching the walls crumble to the trumpetings of victory, not a few have evinced a grim satisfaction in the finality of the rubble pile before them.

Then a strange thing began to happen, an almost incredible thing that made them blink their eyes. The rubble pile began to move. It began to fashion itself into a new fortress, which threatened to be as formidable, as aspiring, as replete with ontological bastions and metaphysical pinnacles as the idealism they had exorcised. And exasperatingly enough, the moving spirit of the new cosmology was not a literary philosopher like the old idealists; he came into philosophy from precisely those quarters which seemed most to discourage such construction; he was himself one of the founders of the new logic and theoretical physics; I mean Alfred North Whitehead.

It would be idle to attempt in a moment or two the picture of one of the most technical and, I am afraid, most obscure, of modern metaphysical systems. Suffice it to say that Whitehead is a philosopher in the grand manner who has described himself as close to idealism. To be sure, he lives in a new world in which substances are abolished and nothing exists but events. This conclusion comes from Einstein. Einstein argued that you cannot assign the place of anything without also giving it a time, and then you have an event. Though the world is made of such things as protons and electrons, these too are really events; so are tables and chairs and mountain ranges, only of rather longer duration. And the great problem of Whitehead is to discover the pattern or laws in accordance with which events affect one another.

Here Whitehead has moved back toward idealism in at least two striking ways. For one thing, he is a panpsychist; nothing for him is dead or mechanical; all things are in a sense alive. Why does a proton attract an electron, or a plant draw some elements and not others from the soil? Such processes are not accidental or mechanical, nor does Whitehead regard them as wholly blind. Every event is an activity, an urge, an endeavor after fuller being; plant and proton alike are showing an elective affinity that is in the end akin to sentience and similar—though at a far remove—to man's selection of food and drink as a means of maintaining life. When an event, or a group of events, achieves a stable pattern of reactions to neighboring events, we have what we call a thing. Things are thus settled ways in which events "prehend" or respond to other events.

Here appears the second way in which Whitehead moved back toward idealism. We saw that, for Royce, to understand anything wholly meant to see its place in the whole. So it is also for Whitehead. He calls his system "the philosophy of organism." To understand a cell in a cabbage we must see the part it plays in the cabbage; to understand the cabbage we must grasp its interplay with soil and light and atmosphere; and these in turn we shall understand fully only when we have fixed their place in the universe at large. The philosophy of the minute philosophers who confine themselves to analysis is therefore in the end self-defeating. You cannot see what things are unless you see them in perspective, and you cannot see them in true perspective until you have widened your vision to take in the whole of things. What you would then see is perhaps more a matter of faith than of clear knowledge, but Whitehead himself has confessed to "the trust that the ultimate natures of things lie together in a harmony that excludes mere arbitrariness."

Thus our story winds back to somewhere near its beginning and proves, like other stories of dubious quality, to have a moral. You can topple over with no great shove the structures of most metaphysicians, even those of the Platos and Hegels, to say nothing of the Royces. What you apparently cannot do is to repress the attempt of the speculative reason to make sense out of its world. You step on it firmly in a Royce only to find after a generation that it is flowering out again in a Whitehead, or in some successor to both. It insists on cropping up in this way because it is not a fad or a passing impulse, but a permanent force in nature. Metaphysics may be, as Bradley suggested, the finding of bad reasons for what we believe on instinct, but he added that the finding of those reasons is no less an instinct. A man who no longer matters tried his hand a few years ago at suppressing this free play of mind; he failed. Stalin seems to be trying it again; he will fail. If Housman is right that "the love of truth is the feeblest of human passions," it remains, nevertheless, a passion, and in some of the best of men a very powerful one. "I love to pursue my reason to an O Altitudo," wrote Sir Thomas Browne. There have always been some men who could say that, and if this brief chapter from the long story of human thought is at all representative, one suspects there always will be.

CHAPTER V

New Forms for Old Faith

George F. Thomas

D URING the years following the First World War, the uppermost religious issue was that between liberalism and fundamentalism. Under the influence of biblical criticism, history of religions, and psychology of religion, liberalism had been quietly developing since the nineteenth century. Biblical criticism, the offspring of historical objectivity wedded to religious sincerity, had reached its maturity after a hundred years of painstaking growth. It seemed to those who had studied the vast amount of evidence unearthed by the scholars that the traditional view of the Bible could no longer be accepted. The Bible, it now appeared, was the record of a long religious and moral development through which the Hebrews had passed from a relatively primitive view of God and his demands upon his chosen people to a lofty ethical monotheism. Doubtless it was the product of acts of divine revelation to inspired men; certainly it contained religious and ethical insights of enduring value. But the later stages of that revelation seemed, with some exceptions, superior to the earlier.

Moreover, the factor of human interpretation was present throughout to color men's understanding of it. Though the essential message was from God, the words, styles, and forms of thought bore the human stamp. Therefore, the books of the Bible could no longer be regarded as all of equal value and identical content. Nor was the Bible inerrant and infallible in every part. For example, it reflected a prescientific view of nature. Obviously, its value lay, not in its scientific opinions, but in its religious and moral wisdom. In short, the traditional assumption that it contained the very words of God communicated by him directly to prophets and apostles by verbal inspiration was no longer tenable. This conclusion seemed to be borne out by the theory of evolution, which gave an account of the origin of species incompatible with the story of creation in the Book of Genesis. However, if the new critical view of the Bible were adopted, such discrepancies between science and Scripture would not need to trouble men's minds. On this view, the story of creation would not be regarded as a scientific account but as a sublime poem affirming the dependence of all natural beings upon God for their existence and value and the preëminence of man over the rest of the creation.

To the liberals the history of religions had made another conclusion inescapable: God had revealed himself to men of other religions also. Had not striking parallels been found between Christianity and the non-Christian religions, e.g., a form of the Golden Rule in Confucianism and the teaching of universal love in Buddhism? The psychology of religion seemed to bear out this conclusion. James B. Pratt[1] and others had shown that religious experiences such as conversion, saintliness, and mysticism are to be found in other religions than those of the West. Of course, the biblical revelation remained unique and final for Christians, but a general revelation in other religions could not be denied. Moreover, was not such a view more consistent with the universal love of God for his children than the narrow view that recognized no salvation outside of Christianity? If so, must not Christians recognize a continuity between their own religious experience and that of other religions, and surrender the arrogant belief that all foreign religions were merely "heathen"?

Similarly, liberals opened their minds to the new truths of science. Instead of watching fearfully every new scientific discovery lest it put up another barrier to faith, they welcomed it as a further step in the conquest of ignorance and a fresh revelation of the wisdom and power of God in the creation. They were equally hospitable to the independent religious thinking of philosophers. If God is one, his truth is one, they argued, and the apparent antagonism between reason and faith must be due to man's limited understanding. Many liberals did not hesitate to revise their faith in the light of what seemed to them the best philosophy available. At the turn of the century, it had seemed to many Christians that in the great systems of idealism from Hegel to Royce the fundamental ideas

[1] *The Religious Consciousness.*

of Christianity had found a more adequate, because more rational, expression. Idealism had interpreted the personal attributes of the biblical God as symbols for an eternal and universal spirit, had stressed the immanence of this spirit in nature and history, and had viewed the incarnation of God in Christ as a perfect example of the union of infinite spirit with the finite spirit in all men. Was not this way of thinking, many asked, less anthropomorphic and arbitrary than that of orthodox Christianity? Though it denied the transcendence and personal character of God, it seemed to make his activity more universal and his presence in nature and human life more real. Moreover, it stressed the uniformity of the divine activity and ruled out occasional divine interferences with natural law in the form of miracles, a view which was more acceptable to modern science because it made God's providence regular and dependable. Above all, it encouraged an optimistic view of man and his moral possibilities. The dark doctrine of an original sin with which every man is born and which limits his moral achievement was put aside. Sin was regarded as a necessary stage in the development of humanity which is progressively outgrown.

Some liberals found in the philosophy of evolutionary naturalism a basis for still more optimistic views of the future of man. Until the First World War and even afterward, Americans accepted almost universally the nineteenth-century doctrine of progress which seemed to be supported by the theory of evolution. The Industrial Revolution, the development of technology, the advancement of science, the growth of democracy and social liberalism, and the extension of education combined with the vast resources and opportunities of America to make high hopes for man's future seem reasonable. In these circumstances it was natural to suppose that orthodox Christianity had exaggerated the suffering of earthly existence and the sinfulness of man. Were not natural evils and sufferings capable of being removed by the progress of science and medicine? Were not the other evils that afflict man largely due to unjust and outmoded social institutions? If so, all that was necessary to overcome these evils was to apply Jesus' teaching about a kingdom of God based on love to the social relationships of man. This was the theme of the social gospel of liberalism, which reached its culmination in the writings of Walter Rauschenbusch early in the century. The historical Jesus became a prophet of social justice, challenging his followers to build the kingdom of God on earth. It was not enough, said Rauschenbusch,[2] to manifest Christian love in personal relationships; love was to be "socialized." As it had already helped to create political democracy, it was now to be applied to the economic and international relationships between groups. Moreover, devotion to the church must cease to be an end in itself and become a means to the transformation of society. In short, salvation was not meant for individuals alone but also for society; and the kingdom was to come on earth as well as in heaven.

[2] Cf. *Christianizing the Social Order* and *A Theology for the Social Gospel.*

Thus, liberalism was much more than a doctrine of progressive revelation in the Bible accompanied by a tolerant attitude toward other religions and a hospitable attitude toward modern science and philosophy. It also brought with it a different emphasis in theology as a whole. It stressed the immanence of God throughout nature and human life; the uniform and unmiraculous working of his providence; the divinity of Jesus as consisting of the union of his human will and purpose with that of God; the ideal of a kingdom of love and justice on earth in social as well as personal life; an optimistic view of man and his moral possibilities; and the subordination of the church to the realization of the kingdom and the development of personality. Liberals recognized that this meant a reinterpretation of many of the doctrines of traditional Christianity. But the enduring values of the gospel spring from a personal experience of God's love in Christ, they argued, and the expression of these in dogmas and creeds must be expected to change with new knowledge. Why should Christians fear change in their dogmas? Christianity is primarily a way of life, not a creed. Did not Jesus himself promise his disciples to send them the Holy Spirit to lead them into all truth?

It is necessary to distinguish carefully between liberalism as I have described it and the modernism which is often confused with it but which is theologically farther to the left. Sometimes "modernism" is used as a synonym for "liberalism" in general, sometimes as a form of liberalism which carries the premises of liberalism to extreme conclusions. This is, to say the least, misleading. Liberalism was and is definitely a continuation of traditional Christian thought and, though it has often been attacked as heretical by orthodox Christians, it has remained within the church. It has always assumed the reality and uniqueness of the divine revelation recorded in the Bible and has put a personal relation to Christ at the center of its religious experience. In other words, its aim has been only to reinterpret the traditional beliefs in the light of modern knowledge without sacrificing them. Modernism, on the other hand, has taken up some position which seemed to be required by the science and philosophy of the time and then has accommodated the biblical point of view to it, retaining only those elements of the latter that seemed to be compatible with the former. It would be unfair to say that the modernist has been more concerned that his faith should be scientifically and philosophically acceptable than that it should be religiously adequate. Modernists have usually been religious men brought up in the church, and in many cases they have remained in the church. But there can be no doubt that they have drunk more deeply than liberals from the wells of modern scientific and philosophical rationalism and have been prepared to give up much of the substance of Christian beliefs.

The reason for this is that modernists have been unwilling to accept a religious belief which cannot be shown to be rational in the modern sense of the term. This unwillingness has led some of them to an attenuated theism.

Believing in the personal God of traditional theism, they have denied or minimized the uniqueness of his revelation in the Bible and his redemptive activity in Christ, though they have retained their belief in the ethical teachings of Jesus and their association with the church. Other modernists have gone still further. They have rejected altogether the belief of traditional theism in a transcendent God with personal attributes who is the creator of the world and who by his providence governs it in accordance with his purpose. Instead, they have embraced a theistic naturalism which has seemed to be verifiable by the empirical method of science and to be in harmony with the philosophical naturalism of our time. According to the most distinguished advocate of this view, Professor H. N. Wieman, God, the source of human good, is to be defined as a process of interaction within nature upon which depends our realization of value. In his terms, God is "the structure of supreme value viewed as possibility of existence, and also that kind of process in nature which most nearly approximates this order of supreme value and promotes further approximation to it."[3] This is not pantheism, since God is not identical with nature as a whole but is a special order or process of nature which makes for the realization of maximum value. Neither is it humanism, since God is more than human ideals and since religious devotion is directed to the source of human good rather than to human good itself. But it differs sharply from liberalism

[3] Essay by H. N. Wieman in D. C. Macintosh, *Religious Realism,* p. 175.

in that God is neither transcendent nor personal but an immanent and impersonal process in nature. Therefore, while traditional Christian beliefs have value as myths adumbrating truth before rational methods of discovery were developed, they must not be regarded as ultimately true.[4] The difference between this view of Wieman's and that of a liberal like Harry Emerson Fosdick is as great as it is clear.

Fundamentalists, in reaction against liberalism, showed considerable strength in the nineteen-twenties. Seeing in liberalism an acute danger to Christianity as a living faith and making no distinction between it and modernism, they attacked it vigorously. Liberals had challenged the "plenary inspiration" and "inerrancy" of the Bible. To the fundamentalists this meant that they were pulling down the pillars of the temple of faith. If the accuracy of the Bible was questioned at *any* point, what was to keep skeptics from denying its claim to contain a divine revelation *altogether?* The Christian faith meant to fundamentalists, not merely a personal experience of the love and mercy of God in Christ, but also the whole series of traditional doctrines derived by orthodoxy from the Bible. Question the Bible at any point, and you are on the way to a complete rejection of it. Question the orthodox doctrines at any point, and the whole structure falls. Against the biblical critics and the liberal theologians, therefore, they de-

[4] Essay by H. N. Wieman in *Religious Liberals Reply.*

fended the Bible as "the infallible rule of faith and practice" and with it the whole system of orthodox doctrines. They insisted upon supernaturalism in an extreme form and defended the authenticity of all the miracles recorded in the Bible. They stressed the full deity of Christ. They put at the center of their preaching the vicarious atonement of Christ on the cross for the sins of men. They rejected the modern optimistic view of man and preached conviction of sin as a necessary condition of salvation. They returned to the otherworldly conception of the kingdom of God and would have nothing to do with the social gospel. Finally, they refused to make any concessions to modern science or philosophy. Religion was a matter of faith in the Word of God and it was presumptuous to test its claims by reason, or reinterpret its meaning in the light of modern knowledge.

But they were not content to defend biblical orthodoxy; they took the battle into the enemy's camp. Liberalism, wrote Professor J. Gresham Machen in 1930, "is not Christianity at all, but a religion so entirely different from Christianity as to belong to a distinct category."[5] Under the influence of modern naturalism, he argued, it has abandoned the "awful transcendence" of God for a pantheistic doctrine of immanence. It has stressed the universal love and fatherhood of God to the exclusion of his justice. It has lost the sense of sin and the recognition of man's need for redemption. Christ has ceased to be an "object of faith"

[5] *Christianity and Liberalism,* pp. 6, 7.

as savior and has become merely an "example of faith," "the fairest flower of humanity" whose faith in God and moral perfection are to be imitated by his followers. In short, liberalism has substituted a moralistic appeal to the will to follow the ideals of the human Jesus for a religion of redemption by Christ the Son of God.

Despite its rigid outlook and intolerant attitude, the appeal of fundamentalism is easy to understand in an age of confusion and uncertainty like ours. Its strength lay not only in the definiteness and intensity of its convictions, but in its recognition of the danger to Christianity from modern scientific dogmatism and philosophical naturalism. The danger was most clearly exemplified by the modernists, but liberals also were not immune to it insofar as they were influenced by the spirit and methods of rationalism. Yet the fundamentalists failed and were bound to fail in their attack upon liberalism. The reason was simple: in their rejection of modernism, they turned their backs on the modern mind. In throwing out the conclusions of a hundred years of devoted work by the biblical critics, they showed that their primary concern was to defend their own fixed conception of Christianity rather than to seek the truth. To the secular mind this was most obvious in their attempt to prevent the teaching of evolution, culminating in the unedifying spectacle of the Scopes trial in 1925. Thus, they seemed to deny the authority of science even in its own proper domain, the *description* of facts. In contrast, liberals could and did

freely admit the authority of science while they insisted
that religion has something very important to say about
the *interpretation* of the facts.

The superiority of liberalism over fundamentalism also
showed itself in the greater fruitfulness of its principles
for the interpretation of the Bible and of traditional doctrines. The fundamentalist was committed by his view of
the inerrancy of the Bible to a defense of positions that
were utterly untenable. How *could* Moses have written
certain parts of the Pentateuch which clearly reflected
conditions of a period hundreds of years after his death?
Did God *really* order the destruction of all the first-born
of the Egyptians and the complete extermination of the
Canaanites? On the other hand, if the Bible was the record
of more than a thousand years of religious and moral
development, as liberals held, errors in authorship and the
presence of primitive conceptions of God here and there
were easy to understand.

With respect to Christian doctrines, the fundamentalist
rejection of new light from modern science and philosophy brought a further nemesis in the form of theological
sterility. A theology that can do nothing but repeat the
orthodox doctrines inherited from the past cannot even
understand and defend them. Theology, like philosophy,
deals in every generation with the perennial issues, and
originality in dealing with them is bound to be limited.
But one thing is certain: theological advances come when
one or a few men of unusual ability and sensitivity are
moved by personal or social crisis of some kind to struggle

with the problems in a fresh and independent way. By this test, the fundamentalists failed to make any advance in theology. One looks in vain for a single new idea or even a new way of putting an old idea in most of their writings. The reason is obvious: they were controversialists defending doctrines rather than theologians thinking about them. The Christian faith constituted no problem for them. They had insulated themselves against contact with all the live intellectual currents of the modern world. As a result, they could not speak to the doubts and difficulties of modern men and women. Even the impending doom of the thirties and the catastrophe of the Second World War have left them, as far as one can see, undisturbed in their dogmatism and unable to speak convincingly to the desperate need of today.

Up to this point, we have been considering religious thought in the twenties and early thirties within the churches. It is necessary now to deal briefly with a third religious movement which arose outside and on the periphery of the churches, religious humanism. Humanism in the religious sense of the term must be distinguished from the literary movement known as the new humanism, which won the support of distinguished literary men like Paul Elmer More and Irving Babbitt, and from Christian humanism such as that of Jacques Maritain. For a time, there was a small number of active and aggressive religious humanists in the Unitarian church and some other Protestant groups. But they are now confined mainly to academic circles, where their influence is considerable.

Professor E. A. Burtt of Cornell University has pointed out in his *Types of Religious Philosophy* that religious humanism in its recent form arose from a conviction of some thinkers that even modernism did not go far enough toward the new world view of naturalism suggested by modern science. To those for whom the scientific method is the sole method of attaining dependable truth, supernaturalism in even the mildest form seems arbitrary. Not only does it rest upon faith in a past revelation rather than upon rational inference from present experience, but also the content of that revelation by its very nature cannot be verified by the scientific method. Moreover, explanation of natural phenomena in terms of final causes or purposes is regarded as unscientific. Therefore, even philosophical theism, which has depended heavily for its proof of the existence of God upon the apparent purposiveness of nature, must be called in question.

But this does not mean that men are left without a religion, since faith may be directed toward humanity and its ideal fulfillment. Man must accept the fact that nature is indifferent to his ideals and values, in the sense that there is no evidence of purpose on her part to realize or support them. But she provides the possibilities of value and conditions for their realization by man. By the adaptation of means to ends through intelligence, ideals can be fulfilled and values attained. The aim of all religions, according to humanists, has been "the good life"; the religious ideal "was always in terms of the highest human values."[6] In the traditional religions, this quest for human values has been associated with dogmas and rites which are not essential to it. The effect of these dogmas and rites has been to encourage the illusion that human ideals must have cosmic support if they are to command our devotion. But the proper object of faith is ideals, not an ultimate reality in which ideals are thought to be eternally anchored and fulfilled. Indeed, whenever faith has asserted that our ideals are guaranteed by a transcendental reality, it has led to otherworldliness and a quietistic acceptance of things as they are. The faith of humanism, on the other hand, encourages men to realize their ideals for themselves through coöperative effort with the aid of scientific intelligence.

John Dewey, in *A Common Faith,* distinguishes between "a religion," which requires specific beliefs and practices, and "the religious," which is simply an attitude toward reality and our ideals in relation to it. All religions, he says, have sought to unify the purposes of the self and to integrate the self with the world as a whole. Through construction by the imagination of an ideal of the self and the world and through devotion to that ideal, this integration can be attained. But since man is a part of nature and is dependent upon forces beyond his control, religious devotion may also be directed toward the relation of the ideal and the actual. This makes possible an idea of "God" in naturalistic terms. This idea, says Dewey,

[6] A. E. Haydon, *The Quest of the Ages,* p. xii.

is "one of ideal possibilities unified by imaginative realization and projection," but it is "also connected with all the natural forces and conditions—including man and human association—that promote the growth of the ideal and that further its realization."[7] Though he recognizes the danger of this idea of God from the humanistic point of view, he thinks that it "may protect man from a sense of isolation and from consequent despair or defiance."[8] He is aware that the religious experience of men has seemed to them to point toward a transcendent God very different from this, but he is confident that that experience has had no evidential value and has merely reflected the religious beliefs men already held.

Is there a place for prayer and worship in religious humanism? Humanists do not seem to agree fully in their answer to this question. One of them doubts that the word "prayer" should be used by them and says that the humanist "derives powers from himself" and "calls upon his own reserves."[9] Another speaks of "self-communion, meditation, reflection," and says that he finds "music, poetry, and a quiet walk into the country effective for that gathering together of oneself that is good for one at times."[10] Still another thinks of worship as an attitude of "veneration" toward that in reality which is most significant for the individual, and speaks of being "touched and lifted by

[7] Page 50.
[8] Page 53.
[9] C. F. Potter, *Humanism, a New Religion*, pp. 17, 18.
[10] R. W. Sellars, *Religion Coming of Age*, p. 280.

natural beauty."[11] "Devotion" to ideal ends and their relation to nature is as close to worship as Dewey seems to come. In short, meditation, veneration for the highest and best, and devotion to the ideal seem to have taken the place of worship in religious humanism.

Why has humanism won the loyalty of a number of thoughtful men during the last generation? The answer is to be found mainly in the tremendous prestige of the scientific method in intellectual circles and the fact that to many it has seemed to make religious belief in the traditional sense arbitrary. In this situation tough-minded men have tried to get along without any conscious faith at all. But the religious impulse has been so strong in men of an idealistic nature that they have had to find a substitute object of faith. In the days of Emerson or even later, when the transcendentalist concept of nature was still strong, it would have been relatively simple for them to turn from God to nature. But during the last hundred years science had destroyed the idealistic view of nature and made it harder to believe in her spiritual character and her beneficence towards man. In an age which had been brought up under the spell of optimistic views of man and his moral possibilities, it was more natural to substitute for the worship of God devotion to man and his ideals. Moreover, the religion of man enabled humanists to break with Christian beliefs and yet to hold on to much of the Christian ethics.

[11] J. H. Dietrich, *Do Humanists Worship?* p. 10.

But humanism has never for long satisfied those whose religious interest has been as strong as their intellectual and ethical interests. It is easy to see why. As Rudolf Otto has shown,[12] religious experience is an experience of the "holy" and the holy is the "numinous" or "mysterious." The "holy" is that which, in Otto's striking phrase, is "wholly other" than objects of ordinary experience. Its presence awakens a sense of "awe" and of one's "creature-liness" before that which transcends oneself. True worship is possible only in the presence of such a transcendent being. Therefore, one may be able to admire, honor, or venerate man and his ideals, but one cannot worship them. It is true that in the presence of some men, e.g., St. Francis or Abraham Lincoln, one may feel a kind of awe or reverence that borders on the religious. But it is because he feels the presence of the divine in them; indeed, it is that presence which separates the saint from other men.

For this reason, the doubt of the plain man whether humanism should be called a religion at all has some justification. Humanism has much in common with ethical culture, which aims at the development of the moral personality, and with humanitarianism, which is moved by compassion and good will for humanity and seeks the welfare of the poor and oppressed. As such, it may be regarded as essentially an ethical and social idealism rather than a religion. But the matter is more complicated than this. For humanists are living in the afterglow of a great

[12] *The Idea of the Holy,* ch. 2.

religious conception of man, that of a spiritual being made in the image of God and entitled to be treated with reverence as potentially a son of God. This Judaeo-Christian conception of man, along with the ethical and social ideals of the Bible, has lingered on in the minds of many who long ago gave up the religious beliefs on which it rests. The "religious" attitude in the form described by Dewey is also the product of the Judaeo-Christian tradition. Therefore, while we may doubt that humanism is really a *religion,* we can hardly doubt that there are *religious elements* in it. The only question is whether these elements can endure for long after the religious tradition from which they were derived has been widely repudiated. On that question, the attitude toward man in countries like Nazi Germany and Communist Russia after that religious tradition was repudiated is not reassuring.

Whatever we may think of the *religious* adequacy of humanism, one of the lessons it can teach us is that *ethical* and *social idealism* must be an integral and important aspect of any religion that is to keep the loyalty of men, and, above all, of men reared under the influence of prophetic Judaism and Christianity. It is a source of shame to religious people in these days that the churches have often tended to forget this fact. Protestants are well aware that this was one of the causes of the reaction against the Orthodox church in Russia. They are only beginning to be aware that the identification of Protestantism with the upper and middle classes and with the white race in this country may produce a similar reaction against it. The social idealism of some of the leading humanists like Dewey, though itself dependent for its origin upon the social ideals of prophetic religion, is a protest against the abandonment of these ideals by conservative Christians. This social idealism is welcomed by those Christians who are convinced that social conservatism is opposed to the true spirit of their faith. Indeed, the best Christians have always known that the love and service of God must show itself above all in the love and service of man, and in that sense they have been humanists themselves.

But this is very far from an admission that devotion to ideals is an adequate expression of religious devotion. The assertion of Dewey that, despite the abandonment of belief in God, the religious attitude can be directed toward human ideals and thus preserved without any real loss is specious. It is false that such a fundamental change in the object of devotion would leave the religious attitude itself unchanged, as the abandonment of worship in the ordinary sense by the humanists clearly shows. A religious attitude has been directed toward objects of many kinds, including natural and human beings. But it has been directed toward them not in and for themselves, but as manifesting the presence of a mysterious and divine power or being. Without belief in such a power or being, it would soon disappear. Moreover, the *kind* of religious attitude varies with the *kind* of religious object. Who would claim that the kind of religious attitude the Canaanites felt toward their Baals or gods of fertility was the same as that the Hebrew prophets felt toward Yahweh, their moral God of justice and mercy?

Again, the humanists' attitude toward human ideals is not the truly religious attitude toward them. The religious attitude differs from the moral attitude toward ideals in that the faith of religion is in the ultimate source of good rather than in the good as such. Whereas morality seeks to realize the good by human effort, religion is centered first and foremost in the cosmic reality from which all possibilities of good spring and which must strengthen our efforts to realize the highest good if they are to bear fruit. Ideals are to be served, but they are never to be worshipped. And they are to be served subject to correction by reference to a more eternal and universal good than our own. If they are served uncritically, they will become the cause of widespread and cruel suffering like the nazi ideal of yesterday and the communist ideal of today.

Finally, the humanists' acceptance of the scientific method as the only method of attaining knowledge about reality seems uncritical and even dogmatic. Natural scientists,[13] as well as philosophers like Whitehead,[14] have made it clear again and again that the scientific method deals only with certain aspects of reality and that other aspects lie outside its province. If so, the assumption of humanists that science rules out the possibility of a spiritual reality transcending the order of natural things and

[13] For example, A. Eddington in *The Nature of the Physical World*.
[14] A. N. Whitehead, *The Function of Reason*.

events in space and time falls to the ground. If humanism has arisen because of the supposed incompatibility of traditional religion with science, as humanists have said, there seems to be no longer any reason to maintain it. There is still a place for it, not as a religion, but as an important element in any truly spiritual and moral religion. As a substitute for religion, however, it will continue to exert an influence over American intellectuals who have rejected or have never been touched by traditional religion.

With all of the three forms of religious thought that have been discussed—liberalism, fundamentalism, and humanism—the writer can claim to have sufficient acquaintance to speak with some measure of confidence. In the case of Roman Catholic thought, however, he can make no such claim because his reading and experience have been too limited. Despite this handicap, he would be doing a grave injustice to an important part of American religious thought if he should be completely silent about it. Perhaps the best course to follow under the circumstances is to deal with a few themes in the writings of some distinguished French and British thinkers of our time: Etienne Gilson, Jacques Maritain, and Christopher Dawson. All three of them have had a wide influence upon American Catholics and considerable influence upon Protestants as well. Moreover, Gilson was for some years a member of the Department of Philosophy at Harvard and Maritain has recently joined the Department of

Philosophy at Princeton, so that their connection with American thought is close.

The first theme that recurs again and again in the French neo-scholastic philosophers is a vigorous defense of reason against the onslaughts of recent irrationalism. According to St. Thomas Aquinas, whose thought is their main source of inspiration, reason has a primary role to play in the life of man. Man is distinguished from the lower animals by his reason and his capacity to choose freely between alternative courses of action after deliberation. His reason is the image of God in him. His highest good, attainable only in the after life with the aid of divine grace, is the intellectual vision of God which will fulfill his desire for truth. Moreover, in this life moral action and social institutions must be governed by rational principles if they are to direct the individual toward and prepare him for this highest good. The emphasis of the Catholic church upon learning and education is largely due to the influence of this way of thinking.

The idea of some Protestants that Catholicism has no place for an autonomous science is erroneous, resting largely upon the attitude of the church authorities to Galileo, Bruno, and others at the dawn of modern science. There have been many distinguished Catholic scientists, of whom Pasteur and Mendel at once come to mind. However, the Catholic church has steadfastly insisted upon the limitation of science to its proper sphere and the necessity for philosophy to interpret the meaning of its discoveries for a world view. As a consequence, it has re-

fused to sanction the modern positivistic tendency to substitute science for wisdom, the description of phenomena
in limited areas for an interpretation of reality as a whole
in terms of first principles. It has also insisted that philosophy must be supplemented by theology, since knowledge
of reality gained by the natural reason alone cannot attain
to truths of the supernatural order necessary to salvation.
In a beautiful essay in his *Science and Wisdom,* Jacques
Maritain has stated the case for such a hierarchy of knowledge leading from the special sciences up to philosophical
wisdom and then to a still higher wisdom through an
alliance of philosophy with theology.

Of course, modern secular philosophers, who are committed to the absolute autonomy of philosophy and ex-
clude any appeal to faith as a source of truth, find this
recognition of the claims of theology unacceptable. But it
is worth noting that every philosophy must take seriously
religious experience and the spiritual insights it brings,
whether it speaks of revelation and faith or not. The effort
of rationalistic philosophers from the time of Descartes to
divorce reason from faith has resulted, as I have shown
elsewhere,[15] in the widespread naturalism and positivism
of today, which have undercut men's ethical and political
as well as religious beliefs. If one seeks to make room for
both reason and faith in his thinking, one is struck by the
wide scope the neo-scholastic position gives to reason in
theology. This is one of the main features of neo-scholasticism which has appealed to many Protestant philos-

[15] G. F. Thomas (editor), *The Vitality of the Christian Tradition,* ch. 9.

ophers and theologians in recent years. At a time when the extremes of philosophical skepticism and theological irrationalism are so strong, its strong affirmation of faith in reason is reassuring. Beyond this, it is a valuable corrective for the intellectual laziness and philosophical indifference of us Americans in general.

The second theme of neo-scholastic thought we wish to discuss is its plea for unity. Professor Gilson's noble appeal at the Harvard Tercentenary in 1936 for a universalism in *thought* that transcends the national pride of thinkers struck a note that has since been heard often in university circles. But it is the appeal for unity in *practice* within the nation and between the nations that has awakened the greatest response in America. In their diagnosis of the disunity of Western civilization, Catholic thinkers are inclined to blame the Protestant Reformation and to find the cure in the return of all Christians to the Roman fold, a view which appeals to few Protestants or secularists. But there is much in their diagnosis that is acceptable to all. They point out, for example, that modern nationalism is a heresy from the Christian point of view, since it tends to make the state the object of an absolute devotion suitable to God alone and denies the unity of his people. Economic and political individualism is no less opposed to Christian principles, since it exalts the individual and his liberties above the common good. The fragmentation of culture reflected in slogans like "art for art's sake" and "business is business" is contrary to the principle that every interest and activity should be devoted to the service of God and the fulfillment of personality as a whole. As a result of our neglect of these Christian principles, our Western civilization is torn by conflicts between nations, classes, and individuals, and our personal lives suffer from an inner disharmony between values. In addition, we have forgotten that common goods have the primacy over private ones, spiritual values over material things, and eternal life over temporal success.

Since the source of our troubles is spiritual and moral, the only possible remedy is a restoration of faith in God as the father of all nations, races, and classes of men; in the moral law established by his will; in the primacy of the spiritual life over material interests; and in the reality of eternal life. But the neo-scholastics are not content to recall men of our secular age to these general religious principles; they also offer specific guidance for the embodiment of these principles in a restored Christian society. This is the third theme in their thinking which has received wide attention in America. Catholic thinkers can never forget that in Europe an approximation to a Christian society was achieved in the thirteenth century under the aegis of the Catholic church, though they realize that we cannot now return to the Middle Ages. Moreover, liberal Catholics like Maritain share the conviction of liberal Protestants that, while Christianity offers eternal salvation to men, it must also concern itself with the conditions of society and culture which during this earthly pilgrimage may further or hinder man's attainment of salvation.

During its long and varied experience in dealing with the world, the Catholic church has developed a social philosophy to which Protestant churches can offer nothing quite comparable. Appealing to the principles of this social philosophy, several of the popes in the last few generations have issued papal encyclicals to guide Catholic thinking and action in dealing with social problems. These encyclicals have been widely circulated and taught in this country, and American Catholics like Father John Ryan have used them in their appeals for liberal economic and social changes. Catholics, like Protestants, tend to be more conservative on economic matters in this country than they are in postwar Europe. But though we should not exaggerate the influence of the social liberalism of the encyclicals and of thinkers like Maritain on American Catholicism, it must not be overlooked.

One of the basic tenets of Catholic social philosophy is that all man-made laws must be consistent with the principles of a universal moral law which is known as the "natural law." Apprehended by the reason of man, this "natural law" is the basis of those natural rights which protect individuals and minorities from the tyranny of the majority. Catholics believe that the conception of rights guaranteed by natural law is one of the great contributions of Catholic social thought to democracy. If belief in natural law is abandoned, they hold, the rights of man will be jeopardized since they will rest upon nothing more dependable than the variable will of the majority or of a dictator.

Among the natural rights of man is that of private property. It is for this reason that Catholic thinkers condemn socialism in all its forms. But they also condemn the economic individualism of unregulated capitalism on the ground that it has destroyed the unity of society by arraying individuals and classes against one another. Therefore, Catholic thinkers like Hilaire Belloc, Jacques Maritain, and Father John Ryan have advocated a much wider distribution of property and the economic and social legislation necessary to bring it about. Some, notably Maritain in his *True Humanism,* have gone so far as to defend profit-sharing and even participation in the management of industry on the part of the workers. Thus, liberal Catholics are seeking a middle way between unregulated capitalism and socialism.

In the sphere of culture, the doctrine of rights based on natural law is used to defend the right of the family and the church against the claim of the state to control the education of children. Catholics insist upon this right because they are convinced that in a country like ours where the state-supported schools have been secularized, Christian education is possible only in parochial schools. Many Protestants fail to understand this attitude because they take for granted the separation of church and state, the secularization of the schools to eliminate sectarian strife, and the right of the individual to form his own religious beliefs without indoctrination from above. But Catholics have never believed that church and state should be separated in an absolute way, though they have accepted the necessity of religious toleration in a country of many churches like ours. They hold that the state must be based upon the acceptance of moral law and should support the efforts of the church to inculcate moral habits and principles in its youth. They are also convinced that religious belief is not a merely personal matter and that children must be instructed in religion early if they are to make it an integral part of their lives. Therefore, in order to maintain the moral foundations of society and to insure the passing on of the religious tradition to the younger generation, they argue that the state should regard the parochial schools as allies of democracy and should support them in suitable ways.

In passing, it may be pointed out that many Protestants have been shaken in their belief in the absolute separation of church and state by the rapid growth of religious illiteracy and the sharp decline of moral standards in the last generation. The recent decision of the Supreme Court ruling out religious instruction by the churches in the public schools has caused large numbers of Protestants to wonder whether such an absolute separation is really required by our Constitution and whether it is not resulting in a collapse of spiritual and ethical standards on an enormous scale. Thus, the differences between Catholics and many Protestants with respect to religious education may be modified somewhat in the near future by a change in the attitude of Protestants. But the Catholic conception of religious education, as expressed in the papal encyclical "On the Christian Education of Youth," differs radically from the Protestant. According to the encyclical, a Christian school is one in which not only religion but all other subjects are taught by Catholic teachers in harmony with the Christian faith. Since the Catholic church is the custodian of the true faith, it should supply the teachers and determine what is taught. Moreover, the young should be protected from evil books, moving pictures, and other amusements. Finally, coeducation is condemned. The extent to which the freedom of philosophers and other professors in Catholic colleges is limited by these principles, I do not know. But it is clear that in school and college alike there is a radical difference between Catholic and Protestant conceptions of what a Christian education should be.

With respect to political issues, there seems to be a tendency among Catholic thinkers to seek a middle course between individualistic democracy and authoritarianism. In the light of the Pope's favorable attitude toward democracy in a recent Christmas message, Protestants have been greatly perplexed by the apparent inconsistencies in the policy of the Vatican in dealing with foreign governments in recent years, particularly its support of Franco in Spain. To understand this, one must bear in mind that the Catholic church is not committed to any one form of government, and that as an international organization it must try to live on some terms with all kinds of govern-

ments. All that it is bound to insist upon is its own freedom to carry out its religious and educational functions
without interference by the state. Beyond that, it welcomes
positive support from governments when it can be had
and naturally tends to favor a government that maintains
its privileges.

American Catholics have been strongly influenced by
democracy and as a minority group defend civil liberties
against government encroachment. Many Protestants,
however, are not convinced that Catholics would continue
to advocate religious liberty if they became a majority.
One thing is certain: Whatever may be its real belief about
democratic liberties, the attitude of the Catholic church
to communism is one of uncompromising hostility, not so
much on economic as on religious and moral grounds. In
his recent book, *Communism and the Conscience of the
West,* Monsignor Fulton Sheen sees communism as a
product of the individualism and materialism of the Western world, and hence as a judgment we have brought
upon ourselves by our abandonment of Christianity.

Arising in this country in the late twenties but exerting
a strong influence only after the coming of Hitler to
power in 1933, the theological movement known as Protestant neo-orthodoxy has stimulated theological thinking
in Protestant circles as nothing else has done since the
rise of liberalism at the end of the last century. It sprang
from the thought of two brilliant Swiss theologians, Professor Karl Barth of Basel and Professor Emil Brunner of

Zurich, though it also owes much to the remarkable Danish literary man and philosopher of a century ago, Sören Kierkegaard. Barth has never come to this country but has been widely read by Americans. Brunner spent a year before the recent war as professor at Princeton Theological Seminary, and is well known to American audiences and readers. By far the most powerful American voice speaking in behalf of neo-orthodox doctrines is Professor Reinhold Niebuhr of Union Theological Seminary. Niebuhr, however, is a brilliant thinker in his own right and is in several respects not typical of neo-orthodoxy. The movement is still confined mainly to the seminaries and to the theologically minded ministers, but it has also made an impression upon the universities, mainly through the writings, lectures, and sermons of Reinhold Niebuhr. His *Nature and Destiny of Man* has been widely read by philosophers, and his *Christianity and Power Politics* and *The Children of Light and the Children of Darkness* have been used as textbooks in courses in political science. It will not do, therefore, to dismiss neo-orthodoxy as an exotic and dangerous foreign growth fed by the disillusionment following the First World War and appealing only to a few reactionary theologians, though there are some who hold that it has already reached the high point of its influence and is ceasing to be a dominant force in contemporary theology.

To the undiscriminating, neo-orthodoxy may seem at first sight to be only a brand of fundamentalism because it also is in sharp reaction against liberalism and appeals to the Word of God in the Bible as the ultimate authority for faith and practice. Like fundamentalism, it also repudiates every alliance of theology with philosophical idealism or naturalism, insisting that the source of religious truth is divine revelation rather than human reason. But neo-orthodoxy differs sharply from fundamentalism in that it accepts the methods and conclusions of biblical criticism. In addition, there is a radical difference between its attitude and that of fundamentalism toward Christian theology. Whereas fundamentalists have tended to neglect historical theology and to go directly to the Bible for their doctrine, neo-orthodox Protestants tend to interpret the Bible in the light of the Protestant reformers, Luther and Calvin, and of St. Augustine. Because of their willingness to learn from modern biblical critics and from the great theologians of the past, their criticisms of liberal theology have been more penetrating than those of the fundamentalists.

Just as the Hebrew prophets denounced their people for apostasy to the gods of the Canaanites and Assyrians, so Karl Barth chastises modern men for their idolatry in putting reason, the state, culture and, above all, man himself in the place of God. Just as the prophets warned their people of the crisis in which they stood and of the divine judgment which was imminent, so Barth warns Christians of today that God is the lord of life and that all their personal achievements are under his judgment. Barth insists again and again that God is transcendent. Modern liberalism and idealism have seen God as immanent in

nature and human life. As a result, Barth holds, they have
confused him with his creatures and forgotten the majesty
and holiness which exalts him above them. This is the
source of their idolatry of themselves and the products of
their own minds and wills. In violent reaction against this,
Barth insists that God is "wholly other" than man and
that any notion of the actual or potential divinity of man
is blasphemous. In doing so, he is recalling men to the
theocentric point of view of early Protestantism and of
the Bible itself.

It is not, however, the full-fledged humanism outside
the churches which is the object of his most biting criticism; it is the half-concealed humanism he finds in the
liberalism within the churches. This is evident, he thinks,
in the confidence of liberals in human reason as a judge
of religious truth, and in the efforts of the human will to
attain goodness by itself. Barth uncompromisingly attacks
these tendencies of liberalism to rationalism and moral-
ism, on the ground that they encourage human pride and
obscure the necessity of divine revelation and redemption
for man. He opposes to them the intense conviction that
God has disclosed himself to man once and for all in
Christ. Moreover, the Word thus revealed must be accepted by faith and obedience alone. All attempts of liberal theologians to demonstrate the faith or even to make
it more palatable to reason are futile. There is no bridge
from the experience and reason of the natural man to
faith, for faith rests upon God's encounter with man in
Christ, and that alone. The appearance of the Eternal at

this one point of history is paradoxical and nothing must be done to lessen the paradox. The incarnation, like the cross, has always been and will always be "folly" and a "stumbling block" to men of the world. "For the foolishness of God is wiser than men," as St. Paul said, "and the weakness of God is stronger than men."[16]

Thus, the key to the Continental neo-orthodoxy is to be found in its uncompromising insistence upon the absolute sovereignty and transcendence of God, the crisis in which man and all his efforts stand under the judgment of God, God's incomprehensible revelation of himself in Christ once and for all for man's redemption, and the necessity to accept his Word by faith alone. In America, however, the aspect of neo-orthodoxy which has had the widest appeal has been its doctrine of man and his sinfulness. Up to the early thirties, Americans had retained their boundless confidence in man and his ability by his own efforts to overcome every evil that confronted him. Since the decline of puritanism in the eighteenth century, they had paid little attention to those who had spoken of an original sin with which man is born and which corrupts his highest achievements. They had accepted the more optimistic doctrine of the Age of Reason and the Romantic movement that man is naturally good, that the evils from which he suffers are due to ignorance or social institutions, and that these evils can be removed by education and social reform. But beginning with the Great Depression and the rise of Hitler to power, our optimism

[16] I Corinthians 1:25.

about man and his possibilities received one rude shock after another. The effect of the series of events that culminated in the Second World War upon idealistic Americans was one of profound disillusionment.

Reinhold Niebuhr had already broken with his earlier liberalism. In *Moral Man and Immoral Society,* published in 1932, he argued that the collective relations between races, classes, and nations are determined primarily by the struggle for power and that a rough justice based upon an equilibrium of conflicting forces is all that can be expected. In 1940, as the clouds of war gathered over America, Niebuhr wrote *Christianity and Power Politics.* Criticizing Christian pacifists, he insisted that Christians cannot escape the necessity of choosing between the evil of war in defense of liberty and the greater evil of tyranny. If the perfectionism of the pacifists prevented them from choosing war, they would succeed only in helping injustice to triumph on a world-wide scale. He maintained that the wisest position for a Christian to take in political issues is that of a realism which avoids both sentimental optimism and hard cynicism about man. In a fine little volume of sermons, *Discerning the Signs of the Times,* he has shown since the war's end how far he is from the complete cynicism with which he is sometimes charged. He preaches forgiveness toward the Germans, repentance for our share in the common guilt that led to the war, and the necessity for patience and self-criticism in resolving our differences with Russia.

The theory of man which lies behind Niebuhr's views

on political and international issues was brilliantly stated
in his Gifford Lectures, *The Nature and Destiny of Man,*
probably the most significant American work on theology
for over a generation. He attacks modern naturalistic
views of man as too cynical; romantic and rationalistic
views as too idealistic. Only the biblical conception, he
argues, does justice to all sides of man's complex nature.
On the one hand, man is a *creature,* involved in the finite-
ness and mortality of all natural beings. On the other
hand, he is preëminent because he alone of natural beings
has been made in the *image of God.* This is why as a
spiritual being he can transcend himself and unite himself
by faith with the eternal ground of all existence and value.
Thus, man is neither brute nor angel, neither mere animal
nor pure spirit, but a being who stands "at the juncture of
nature and spirit." This is the source both of his greatness
and of his tragedy—of his greatness because his freedom
may be creatively used to serve the purposes of God; of
his tragedy because he does not use it so.

This leads Niebuhr to the third aspect of the biblical
view: man as *sinner.* His penetrating analysis of the nature and forms of sin has been very widely discussed and
has had great influence upon religious thinking. Though
his inspiration for it has been derived from St. Paul, St.
Augustine, and the Reformers, the effect of modern psychology and of his own keen observation is everywhere
apparent. Man's sin is occasioned by the insecurity and
anxiety he feels as a finite being involved in the contin-
gencies of nature. This anxiety does not lead him into sin

by necessity, since he might gain a sense of security by faith in God. In actuality, however, he seeks to reassure himself by various forms of pretension, deceiving himself that he can raise himself above his insecurity by claiming absoluteness for himself or for something of his own. This pretension is the cardinal sin of pride. It is by virtue of the spiritual rather than the animal element in him that the sin of pride arises, as St. Augustine said long ago. Man's supreme tragedy is that his highest faculty, which was meant to be the source of his creativity, becomes the source of his downfall. Pride takes many forms, individual and collective. Not only the will to power, which is the easiest form of pride to detect, but the subtler and more hidden forms of intellectual, moral, and spiritual pride are depicted by Niebuhr in vivid terms. Even sensuality, which arises primarily from a desire to escape from responsible freedom, is often itself an expression of pride, as in the will to power of the sexual adventurer.

Thus, man is a spiritual being made in the image of God, but he is also—and universally—a sinner. Though his sin is not a necessity of his nature and condition, Niebuhr asserts, somewhat paradoxically, that it is inevitable. The doctrine of original sin does not depend for its validity upon the historical authenticity of the fall of Adam in the Garden. What the doctrine expresses is the insight that every particular sin a person commits, however early in his childhood, seems to spring from a will that is already sinful or, as Niebuhr puts it, "sin posits (i.e., presupposes) sin." Moreover, sin is not confined to the

unregenerate man, as Christian perfectionists often seem
to think; it also persists in the life of the redeemed. To the
end of his life, the Christian must struggle with sin; to the
end he will be unable to attain the perfection or holiness
he seeks.

The implications of this for Christian ethics and politics
are far-reaching. It means that, while Jesus' ethic of love
must guide the Christian in all his decisions, the remnants
of egoism and pride in him will corrupt his motives and
even his actions in some degree. Hence, the appropriate
attitude for him will always be repentance and humility
before God. He will need not only to forgive, but also to
be forgiven by, his fellows. In politics, it means that he
must abandon utopianism of every kind, for collective
egoism is even more difficult than individual to master by
love. At the most, he can achieve relative but not absolute
justice, choosing the better of two goods or the lesser of
two evils. Therefore, though Niebuhr has always been a
strong believer in the social application of Christian ethics
and has taken an active part in politics as a Christian
socialist, he differs from the social gospel of liberalism in
that he has no utopian illusions about socialism or any
other social or political reform. Since the human factor of
sin will remain under any social system, social evils are
sure to arise. Communists share the social utopianism of
almost all modern thought in their implicit faith that the
elimination of capitalism will lead to a classless society in
which all social evils will disappear. Yet in Russia the
elimination of the evils of capitalism has brought in its

train the evils of bureaucracy and dictatorship by a new ruling class.

Moreover, if we abandon utopianism, we shall have to have a more realistic defense of democracy than we have had in the past. We have assumed that men, under the influence of sympathy and reason, will voluntarily bring their conflicting individual and group interests into harmony. This assumption rests upon a too optimistic view of man, Niebuhr argues in *The Children of Light and the Children of Darkness*. Man as a moral being has enough desire for justice to make democracy possible, but as a sinner he has enough egoism and will to power to make democracy necessary. The strongest argument for democracy, on these terms, is that only democracy can preserve a measure of freedom and encourage the initiative of individuals and at the same time curb their irresponsible use of their freedom and the will to power of their rulers.

Finally, this realistic doctrine of man implies a philosophy of history which Niebuhr has as yet only suggested in broad outline. The liberal doctrine of progress toward an earthly state of perfection and happiness is illusory. Man is capable of relative improvements, e.g., the achievement of democracy in the Western world. But his freedom makes it possible for him at every stage of development to realize evil as well as good, and his sin makes it inevitable that he will do so in some form. Thus, history cannot redeem itself, but needs a redeemer. The full depth of the Christian faith in redemption through Christ and of the Christian hope for eternal life becomes

apparent only in the light of man's inability to fulfill his
moral possibilities in history.

As yet Niebuhr has not attempted to develop a doctrine
of Christ, redemption, and eternal life. This is the source
of the frequent criticism leveled against him by some
Christians that he has brought man once again to realize
the depth of his need for divine grace, but has not shown
him how that need has been and still can be met by Christ.
In this respect, he is like many another American Christian, who has been taught by the tragic events of our time
that he can no longer rest his hopes upon man but has
to win his way back to a vital faith in God's redemptive love in Christ. But what he and other neo-orthodox
thinkers have done—and it is much—is to challenge the
dominant liberalism of a generation ago, to show that the
biblical revelation contains profound insights into the nature, possibilities, and limitations of man, and to demonstrate that these insights are more illuminating than modern naturalism and idealism for an understanding of the
social problems which confront us.

The disillusionment of the thirties was deepened during
the years of the Second World War when man's inhu-
manity to man and his betrayal of the highest ideals of
Western civilization awakened a sense of horror everywhere. The growing influence of neo-scholasticism and
neo-orthodoxy alike has been partly due to fear that our
civilization may be disintegrating before our eyes. But it
has also been due to a growing awareness that our personal

lives have been emptied of meaning and dignity by the loss of religious and moral conviction during the period between the two world wars. We have been lacking in a sense of direction, without a purpose to possess us and a passion for something of absolute worth. We have discovered that humanistic devotion to ideals and values of our own making does not satisfy our aspiration for a universal and perfect good which transcends our limited and imperfect goods and at the same time gives them meaning. Even the liberalism of the twenties has come to seem inadequate because of its mild manner and its defensive attitude in setting forth the claims of Christian faith and love. Are the sweetness and light of the old liberal Christianity, we ask, an adequate substitute for the intense and single-minded faith which moved ancient martyrs to pour out their blood, produced medieval saints and mystics, gave courage to the Reformers, and brought about the Great Awakening and the world-wide missionary movement of the last century?

This has led to a complete abandonment of liberalism by a number of theologians, especially younger men. But the typical reaction against liberalism in theological circles has been less extreme. Almost all liberals have been affected by neo-orthodoxy, but few have been completely converted by it. In 1939, after neo-orthodoxy had become well known in this country, the editor of *The Christian Century* asked a number of Christian thinkers to write their spiritual autobiographies for the last ten years and to record the major changes in their religious thinking.

All or almost all showed that they had had to take serious account of neo-orthodoxy. Among the most significant articles was one by Professor John Bennett, now of Union Theological Seminary. One change he recorded in his thinking was a new interest in the Christian tradition as a corrective of his earlier religious individualism. But he was "more repelled than helped by the Barthian form of traditionalism," he wrote, because of its "limitation of revelation to the Bible" and its "absolutizing of the canon of the Scripture" and "the theology of the Reformers."[17]

In similar vein, Professor Robert Calhoun of Yale Divinity School wrote: "Special revelations . . . have always needed to be checked by some more general frame of reference: the written Scriptures coolly and historically studied, the traditional and common experience of the church, and the still more general experiences and tested beliefs of mankind." Thus, like Bennett, he rejected the extreme biblicism of neo-orthodoxy. But he confessed also that he had been driven to recognize that "theology cannot get on without special revelations," and that "it must start from such revelations, above all from those which center about Jesus Christ and the faith which they evoke." "This amounts," he added, "to a Copernican change in my orientation. With it has come a new sense of the special significance . . . of the Bible, the creeds, theological tradition and the Christian church." We must not, he concluded, cease to apply to these "the principle of relevance or coherence which is basic to all rational living," but "in

[17] *Christian Century*, Feb. 8, 1939.

their presence our logic seems clearly to have neither the first nor the last word."[18] Both Bennett and Calhoun also acknowledged a change from a rather naïve optimism about man and his moral possibilities to a more "sober and chastened view of the human problem." But this means "moral realism," said Bennett, not "cynicism or even pessimism." Though "sin is a universal and permanent factor in human life . . . we can have great faith in human possibilities, in what God can do with men whose hearts are open to his influence."[19] Professor Walter Horton of Oberlin University expressed himself in somewhat similar fashion in his article, which bore the significant title "Between Liberalism and the New Orthodoxy."

In these articles by Bennett, Calhoun, and Horton nearly ten years ago is expressed a new theological attitude which has been steadily growing since that time and which seems to many to point the way American religious thought should follow in the next generation. This attitude has been influenced by the brilliant insights of Professor Paul Tillich of Union Theological Seminary. In certain respects the thinking of Reinhold Niebuhr is closer to it than to neo-orthodoxy, and his brother, Professor Richard Niebuhr of Yale Divinity School, may be regarded as a distinguished representative of it in many ways. It has been called "religious realism," mainly because of its realistic theory of knowledge and its repudiation of the optimistic view of man of the older liberalism.

[18] *Christian Century,* May 31, 1939.
[19] *Christian Century,* May 17, 1939.

That term is not adequate because it expresses only one aspect of the new attitude. What is equally characteristic of it is its attempt to do justice to the traditional insights revived by neo-orthodoxy and at the same time to retain the essential elements of value in the liberalism of the last two generations. In this sense it may be regarded as a "mediating" type of theology, and some of its representatives have been influenced by British theologians of the *via media* like Archbishop William Temple. Most of all, however, it aspires to develop theology which will do justice to the major insights of the Bible and the great theologians of the past, but in terms relevant to the modern situation. In other words, its representatives believe that theology is important enough to be taken very seriously and that those who wish to make a real contribution to it must free themselves from uncritical allegiance to any particular school of thought and try to think for themselves about the perennial problems. Though this new movement has as yet found no single American spokesman to give it adequate expression, it is represented by a number of men in two theological discussion groups, one composed of older and the other of younger members. From the first of these groups there has already come a volume edited by President Henry Van Dusen of Union Theological Seminary with the title *The Christian Answer;* from the second there will soon appear a volume on the thought of St. Augustine. What do the representatives of this new movement stand for?

First, they share the conviction that there has been a

special revelation from God in the series of historical events culminating in Christ, and that this revelation is ultimate. They gladly accept the fact that there has also been a general revelation of God in nature, history, conscience, and other religions. They also take for granted the critical method of studying the special revelation recorded in the Bible, as well as the testing of its insights by further religious experience and by reason. They believe, in Calhoun's words, that in relation to this revelation "our logic seems clearly to have neither the first nor the last word." The historical revelation in the Bible is an objective reality *given* to men in faith, and, though it must be interpreted by reason, its validity can neither be proved nor disproved by the known canons of reason. At this point, the new movement, though it accepts biblical criticism, is less rationalistic than the older liberalism. On the other hand, it is opposed to rigid orthodoxy in doctrine, fundamentalist or otherwise, holding that the full meaning of the biblical revelation cannot be exhausted by dogmas and creeds, important as these are for the life of the church. Archbishop Temple says that God revealed *himself,* not *dogmas about himself.* Since his revelation came in concrete historical events and above all in a person, it can never be expressed completely by the abstract concepts of theology or philosophy.[20] Thus, the Bible brings us into living contact with God and his will for us, but it is not a collection of dogmas that solves all our religious problems or moral rules that can be me-

[20] William Temple, *Nature, Man and God,* Lect. XII.

chanically applied in our decisions. Our attitude toward
it must, therefore, be one of faith in the Word contained
in it, but must also be discriminating in the interpretation
and application of the words in which it is expressed.

Second, the new movement stands for what Bennett
calls "moral realism" but not "cynicism or even pessimism" in its doctrine of man. It accepts the fact, stressed
by neo-orthodoxy, that man is a sinner and will never
eliminate sin from his personal and social life. But it also
takes seriously the biblical doctrine of the "image of God"
in man and insists that sin has obscured but not destroyed
it. Thus, Bennett speaks of "the integrity, the selfless and
humble devotion, and the courage of countless persons."
Moreover, it is reluctant to "set rigid limits to the range of
the divine grace,"[21] as neo-orthodoxy sometimes seems to
do, for those representing the new movement believe that
the redemptive love and mercy of God must not be lost
sight of in stressing his judgment. Thus, Walter Horton
speaks of God as exercising his providence with his left
and his right "hands," one of law and judgment, the other
of grace and love.[22] Furthermore, though the new theologians are aware of the danger of ethical perfectionism,
many of them are convinced that the ideal of perfection
or holiness is an integral element in the Christian ethic,
though no one should be so self-righteous as to think that
he has attained it. Therefore, nothing in their thinking
contradicts the possibility of saintliness or the importance

21 *Christian Century*, May 17, 1939.
22 *Realistic Theology*, pp. 112, 113.

of the devotional life in developing it, as Professor Douglas Steere of Haverford College has described it in his fine little book *On Beginning from Within*. But the tragedy of human life is precisely the fact that even noble impulses such as loyalty and self-sacrifice and religion itself are often perverted to evil ends by pride and egoism, as in the case of the Nazi soldier or the persecutor of heretics during the Spanish Inquisition. Therefore, the new theologians unequivocally reject the humanistic tendency of the modern world to think that man can save himself without the aid of divine grace.

Third, representatives of the new movement agree with the older liberalism on the importance of the social gospel, but they interpret it in the light of the realism about man we have just described. They have abandoned social utopianism and are insisting upon a more adequate theological basis for the social gospel. Some of them believe that Protestantism has been weakened in its social ethic by its neglect of the problem of justice and law. Protestant social thinkers have tended to reject the Catholic conception of natural law as a Stoic importation into Christian thought and have depended upon a direct application of Jesus' teaching about love to social problems. As a result, Emil Brunner in his recent *Justice and the Social Order* says flatly that for three hundred years Protestants have been without a theory of justice. It is now recognized that, if Christian love is to be socially effective, it must be expressed in social institutions, patterns, and laws based upon principles of justice. Accordingly a resolute attempt is being made to define Christian principles of justice which can guide men in their decisions on social policy. Notable in this connection are a recent volume by Professor Eduard Heimann, *Freedom and Order,* and another by Professor John Bennett, *Christian Ethics and Social Policy.* Others have pointed out that the Protestant churches have compromised with an unjust and materialistic social order in their economic practices, their racial discrimination, and their general social conservatism. One of the strongest indictments of our culture as a whole and of the complacency of our churches is to be found in a small volume edited by Clarence Craig under the title *The Challenge of Our Culture.*

Fourth, in spite of this critical attitude toward the churches, the new theologians have rediscovered the importance of the church. The castigation of the churches as they *are* for their involvement in our unjust society is itself due to a growing realization of what they *should be.* Christianity has always been more than a set of religious beliefs and ethical ideals; it has been an historical movement bringing a new life to men, and it has made its impact upon the world through a religious community. Liberals in the twenties were inclined to think of religion as a personal affair and to regard the church as a means to their personal development. The continuity of the church with the past, its rich tradition, and the necessity of its solidarity in the face of hostile powers were little recognized. The stern realities of the world situation in the thirties and during the Second World War forced men to a radical revision of this individualistic attitude toward the church. They came to see that they were dependent upon it for the religious experience they enjoyed, that they needed the church to nourish their faith in God in a time of disillusionment with man, that Christians must stand together in the face of persecution abroad and indifference at home. Moreover, Christians saw in the heroic resistance of the church to the Nazis in Germany, Norway, Holland, and elsewhere a proof of vitality that had not been expected. Men in the armed services discovered what Christian missions had meant to the Orient, even in small islands of the Pacific. Meanwhile, Protestant churches for the last two decades have been trying to find a way to overcome their divisions and the narrow sectarianism that has prevented them from coöperating in many fields of common endeavor. The movement for church unity which is known as the "ecumenical movement" has given rise to a number of remarkable world Christian conferences, and has stimulated several successful efforts at organic union between Protestant churches, notably in Canada and South India.

For these and other reasons, the new theology we are describing manifests a deepened appreciation of the church. There has been no tendency to gloss over the defects of the actual churches, their ministers, or their lay members—indeed, we have seen that criticism of them has been very sharp—but the ideal church, the church as it might be, has played a prominent part in recent thinking. Also, Christian thinkers have become more aware both of the importance of the church as a world institution and of the shamefulness of the denominational differences which prevent them from making their common witness more effective at home and abroad. The major developments within theology more and more cut across denominational lines. It has seemed clear for some years that a new consensus of theological thinking is emerging among the Protestant churches and that theologians of each denomination are more conscious of their loyalty to the church as a whole than to their own branch of it. The new theology is, therefore, definitely an ecumenical theology speaking for the whole church.

Thus the new theological movement is taking the Bible very seriously, though not uncritically; it is adopting a realistic but not a pessimistic view of man and his moral possibilities; it is seeking a more adequate social expression of love in terms of justice; and it is aware of the great importance of the church as well as the serious defects of the churches. One must mention, finally, the renewed effort to come to terms with the central mystery of the Christian faith, the nature of "the great enigma" Christ and of the redemptive work of God in and through him. For example, three recent small books[23] on Christ by Professor John Knox of Union Theological Seminary seem to be pointing the way to a new mediating position between the orthodox and the liberal conceptions of him.

[23] *The Man Christ Jesus,* 1941; *Christ the Lord,* 1946; and *On the Meaning of Christ,* 1947.

As one tries to get a perspective upon the American religious thought of today, one cannot help feeling that we are becoming more mature in our theological thinking. We are still dependent upon Europe for much of our inspiration. But we are not following along behind uncritically; we are thinking for ourselves. It is a good sign that our hitherto activistic and practical American Christianity is beginning to be more reflective. Serious Americans have not for generations taken theology as seriously as they are taking it today. Though there is still plenty of unenlightened obscurantism and emotionalism, as in the pentecostal and millenarian sects, we are more aware of the necessity of wisdom and sanity in religion than before. Universities have an important role to play in the attainment of that breadth and depth of understanding which are of the essence of religious wisdom. Some would say that religion is a precious flower that flourishes and sheds its fragrance abroad only in the darkness, and that it withers in the light cast upon it by reason. I do not subscribe to that view. Surely God wants us to love him with our whole selves, our minds as well as our hearts and souls. But religious thought presupposes religious faith and experience, and it is our besetting sin in academic circles to suppose that reason needs nothing but itself. What we really need, as John Wesley said, is to unite "knowledge with vital piety." Our age is crying out for just such a union to give meaning once more to our personal lives and to redeem our civilization from its spiritual and moral decay.

DATE DUE